I FORGOT TO CRY

Breast Cancer and How One Woman
Embraced Her Journey to Healing

CLAUDEAN NIA ROBINSON

iUniverse, Inc.
Bloomington

I Forgot to Cry
Breast Cancer and How One Woman Embraced Her Journey to Healing

iUniverse books may be ordered through booksellers or by contacting:

iUniverse
1663 Liberty Drive
Bloomington, IN 47403
www.iuniverse.com
1-800-Authors (1-800-288-4677)

ISBN: 978-1-4759-1937-0 (sc)
ISBN: 978-1-4759-1938-7 (hc)
ISBN: 978-1-4759-1939-4 (ebk)

Library of Congress Control Number: 2012908141

Printed in the United States of America

iUniverse rev. date: 06/08/2012

DEDICATION

This book is dedicated in loving memory to my parents, Mr. Jesse Thomas and Mrs. Jessie Winifred Cushinberry. I thank God for choosing them to be my loving parents, my rocks, and my confidants; they were just wonderful, kind-hearted people to have in my life. Knowing that my parents were watching over me was a comfort during my battle with cancer.

My parents made me strong, loving, caring, and giving. Without the words of wisdom and encouragement they shared with my siblings and me, I could not have been the warrior I was during my journey. The values they instilled in me have carried me through many trials and tribulations. I have passed along these same values to my sons, Warren Jerome and Allan Michael.

Also I thank God for my brother Jesse Jr. who suddenly left this earthly life many years ago, at the age of seventeen, to join our heavenly Father.

I am truly blessed for being a part of their lives. The strength I needed to embrace my new journey was brought on by the spirits of my parents and brother and by the love of my husband, Jerre, my sons, Warren and Allan, my siblings, Claudette, Dale, Paula, and Wanda, my brother-in-law, Fred, my sister-in-law, Anita, and a host of devoted friends.

I especially dedicate this book to all breast cancer patients and survivors, whose struggle I know all too well. You are the real warriors who inspire and give us hope to live life as if there were no tomorrow.

ACKNOWLEDGEMENTS

First, I must sincerely thank the professionals, especially my oncologist, who provided the excellent medical care critical to the success of my journey. My family, friends, and I will forever be grateful for your service, kindness, and compassion.

My heart belongs to my loving husband, Jerre, and my sons, Warren and Allan. You were with me every step of the way. Your love and encouragement gave me the strength to never give up.

Marlene, I give my deepest appreciation to you for transcribing this book while I was experiencing the peripheral neuropathy that impaired my ability to write. You gave me the jump I needed to move forward and write this book. Thanks, Julbe, for introducing me to Marlene.

Barbara, special thanks to you for helping me through the first edits of my book. Your friendship, strength, humor, and kindness throughout my journey brought me great comfort.

Mark, your expert critiques of my book were invaluable. Thanks, my friend.

Brenda, your profound questions kept me focused on the real purpose of my book, and that was greatly appreciated. Your writing abilities have taught me that there are limitless possibilities for expression.

Caitlin, thanks for wrapping up the final, edited version of this book. Your patience and editing were amazing.

Tony, what can I say? Your artistic talent was right on point for the cover of this book. Thanks for being a friend and for sharing your talent.

Oliver, your excellent photography skills capture the essence of who I have become. Thank you for my author photo.

Also, I offer my heartfelt thanks to the women in Zion Church's small life group called Transition. Your commitment to serve God and to assist and support me during my time of need was very humbling and completely appreciated.

CONTENTS

CHAPTER 1

Where to Begin?

My breast cancer journey began in the wee hours of Friday, February 8, 2008. I had a typical Thursday evening commute, leaving the slow-motion, bumper-to-bumper stress of Washington, DC, and arriving in a neat suburban community in Cheverly, Maryland, where I have lived with my husband and two sons for twenty-seven years. My husband, Jerome or Jerre, is affectionately known as "Byrd." Ever since high school, when he was a member of the track team, all his friends call him Byrd because he used to float like a bird over the high-jump bar. I call him Byrd.

I have been married twice. My first husband was Sam. We were married on June 23, 1973, and relocated to Washington from Kansas because it was his home. We parted amicably as friends after three years, but I decided to stay in Washington because I enjoyed the city. My twin sister, Claudette, also moved to DC about three months after I married Sam, and she has been here ever since. Over the years, I've met lots of wonderful people, including my second husband. We married on August 23, 1980.

When I walked in the door that evening in 2008, I knew I would be home alone. Byrd was called in unexpectedly to work overtime. This happens every once in a while when another computer programmer is out or when a technical problem requires all hands on deck to resolve it.

Our older son, Warren, was no longer living at home. At twenty-six years old, he was living on his own and working as an assistant manager at a nearby car rental service. Our younger son, Allan, was miles away. He was nineteen years old at the time and attending his first year of college in

Virginia. I am not a person who has spent much time alone. Even in the womb, I had company. I was born with a fraternal twin named Claudette in Topeka, Kansas. My name is Claudean Bernice Robinson, known by many as "Nia," but if you grew up with me, you know me as "Deanny."

A lot of people talk about the "empty-nest syndrome," but I loved the peace and quiet of being at home alone, especially after a long, hard week at the office. I came in the door, and I loved the silence. I put my purse and keys on the red, contemporary sofa on the way to the hall closet to hang up my coat. Finally, I could breathe in, relax, draw some water for a cup of peppermint tea, and take it easy in the kitchen, where I always seem to find myself.

Moving through the quiet, enjoying the peace all around me, I took a few sips of tea and climbed the stairs to my bedroom. My bedroom is my sanctuary. Red is my favorite color, but my bedroom is blue. That's where I withdraw to find peace. My magazines are there; my chaise lounge and my music are there—anything I feel like hearing, jazz, R&B, country. It's all in my bedroom. So I sat in the chaise lounge, flipped on the TV to listen to the news, and started looking at the mail and a few of my bills.

I'm not sure how long I was sitting there, but pretty soon I was no longer watching the TV; the TV was watching me. I was so drained from my week at work that I realized I was dozing and managed to climb into bed. I woke up in the middle of the night. I never wear a watch. I don't even set an alarm to go to work in the mornings, but this night I noticed the clock on my husband's side of the bed read 2:30am. Somehow I almost felt driven to go to the bathroom. When I flipped on the light, I looked in the mirror, and for some reason I placed my hand on my right breast and felt a lump about the size of a small acorn. Going to the bathroom in the middle of the night is not unusual for me. I generally take a trip or two during the night, but this particular trip was different. It changed my life forever.

It's funny how your mind races when you are in a space unknown to you. Time froze for me, and a thousand different emotions washed over me all at once. I felt threatened and afraid. I couldn't move. I was filled with the uncertainty of what that moment would mean to me. I was overpowered by fear. Those emotions were so intense that I hope I never experience that again. The impact was so heavy and so powerful.

I remember thinking, *God, why now?* I knew then my life would never be the same. I was about to embark on a new journey. Somehow I knew, but at the same time, I didn't have a clue what was in store for me. Immediately, my mind was flooded with a million questions. I wondered, *God, how much more time will you allow me to spend with my family and friends?*

At that moment, I felt incomplete. In particular, I didn't feel like I had finished raising my youngest son. All I really needed was the opportunity to see my sons mature and become independent, self-sufficient men. I had barely adjusted to Allan being gone, and my fear was that I might not be able to guide him to maturity like I had with his older brother. Warren was maturing nicely. That pleased me. I relaxed some when I accepted that if it was God's plan to transition me from this earth, Warren would be a strong mentor for his younger brother and a comfort to his father.

All of this ran through my mind in a matter of moments. When I felt the lump, I was stunned and I gasped. I had thought I was all alone, but I heard Warren call upstairs from the bottom of the steps. He must have used his key to the basement door, and I didn't hear him come in.

"What's wrong, Mom?" I heard his feet climbing the stairs. He pushed his way into the doorframe of the bathroom where I was still standing looking in the mirror. I turned to him and looked in his face and said, "Warren, Mom just found a lump in her breast."

"Mom, we need to go to the hospital." He was looking surprised and shocked.

I think he sensed fear in me. He was so used to seeing me as strong and in control. He's very sensitive, very perceptive, so I knew he could sense something was wrong with me. His concern made the mother in me take over. I didn't want him to have anxiety about something unknown. I decided to calm down, and I began to put some things in motion.

"Warren, I promise I will call the doctor's office in the morning and make an appointment." He began to calm down and relax once I said that. I also knew that going to the emergency room at that time would take about as long as it would take for the doctor's office to open. Plus, the doctor's office had my history and could be more efficient in determining what was wrong.

I knew I had to call my husband.

I called Byrd at work, and he said, "Hey, what are you doing up?"

"I wanted you to know that I just discovered a lump in my right breast," I said calmly and matter-of-factly.

Byrd is a fairly mellow person. He doesn't get excited very easily. He was calm too, but I sensed worry in his silence.

"Well, I am going to come home." He wanted to come home right away to comfort me.

"No, Warren's here."

"Oh, Warren came home tonight?"

"Yes, we've been talking, and he's such a comfort to me." Byrd knew Warren and I were very, very close, so he felt relieved.

Byrd would get off from work in three more hours. I felt there was no sense in him coming home right away, since he was already scheduled to come home soon.

"I'm fine."

"Okay. Try to get some rest, and I'll be home shortly. I love you," he said, and then we hung up.

Warren came into my bedroom. He sat in the chaise lounge, and I propped myself up in bed with some pillows. We started to talk about his life, and I asked him if he felt there was anything I could do for him. I was trying to reassure myself that the way I had raised him was at least right for him. I wanted to be sure that I wouldn't have to worry about him. I took a chance and asked him whether he thought I had been a good mom.

"Yes, Mom," he said. "You're the best mom I know. I love you." That really made me feel much better.

I asked him what his goals were in life. He told me he wanted to finish his degree in business and that he wanted to own his own marketing business eventually. That gave me a picture of where he saw his life going. I decided to stop there. I didn't want to scare him, so we made a little small talk, and then he drifted off, and I drifted off. He fell asleep on the chaise lounge, and I fell asleep propped up in the bed.

When Byrd arrived home from work that morning, he immediately came upstairs to our bedroom. I was already up and getting dressed for work. Byrd embraced me, and I put his hand on my lump. He lovingly said, "Everything is going to be alright." Byrd trusted that, once my doctor's office opened that morning, I would call and make an appointment as soon as possible.

He asked if I felt like going to work that day. I said, "Yes." In retrospect, Byrd and I recall this moment differently. He thinks I stayed home that day and that we went to see the doctor right away. But, I'm certain that he just couldn't remember that it was actually four days after I discovered the lump before I was seen by a physician. Besides, a lot of time passed between the beginning of my cancer experience and the writing of my experience.

Byrd said, "Hon, take your time going to work, and call me when you get there." He now went into his protective mode. His silent fear was obvious to me, and I reassured him that I'd call as soon as I arrived at work. I don't know how I managed to get to work. The commute seemed to go smoothly that morning. No road construction, no detours, and no bumper-to-bumper traffic. Actually, my mind was not focused on the discovery of my lump. I don't know if I was numb and started going through the motions. At this point, I wasn't emotionally invested in the discovery. There was nothing urgent about what was happening to me.

As soon as I arrived at work, I called Byrd to let him know everything was fine. He understood what that meant without going into any details. He knew that when I said, "everything was fine," I wasn't talking about the commute. Once I settled in my office, retrieving voicemail messages and glancing at my e-mails, I started pulling materials together for a new hiring manager's orientation.

I was a staffing/recruitment manager in the human resources office. Our work was nonstop but very fulfilling because I thoroughly enjoyed the work. Once everything was in order for the orientation, I decided to call Pam, my co-worker and friend. Pam and I worked closely together and traveled as a team on recruitment trips. I told her of my discovery. She was sad to hear it and said, "Call if you need me." Pam, whom I affectionately call "Duckie," sent a book on breast cancer awareness in an interoffice mail envelope a couple of days later. At first, I was confused as to why Pam would think or suggest that I might have breast cancer. I soon realized that she was just being proactive and truly supportive. I had forgotten that Pam lost her mother to cancer many years ago and other family members to the disease as well. Pam's insightfulness was appreciated, and the book was extremely helpful.

My other colleague, Barbara, who worked in the staffing department as well, had not arrived yet, so I confided in her later that afternoon. I also told my goddaughter, who worked in another department. Eventually, my director stopped by my office to share information regarding her executive meeting. I told her of my discovery and that I was waiting for my gynecologist's office to return my message. She nearly panicked and could not believe how cool and calm I appeared. She suggested that I go to a hospital nearby, and I told her I felt more comfortable waiting to hear back from my doctor's office. After all, this lump did not grow overnight and a few more hours would not matter. I continued to float through the day after sharing my discovery. I treated my situation like a matter of fact. Looking back I wonder if maybe I had memory loss about something that most people would find devastating.

My gynecologist's office called me before I left work. Unfortunately, my doctor was out of town, and I was scheduled to see her colleague on Tuesday of the following week. The waiting period for that doctor's appointment was the longest few days I had ever experienced. Over the weekend, I could not find the lump. Apparently, it was a migrating lump. I thought for a moment that I was going crazy. I knew it was there, but where did it go? This was really getting on my nerves!

Finally, after a long, stressful weekend of waiting, I met with the "substitute" gynecologist. I was extremely upset with his bedside manner. I had never seen this doctor before, and he didn't even mention his name. I learned who he was when I read the medical report later on in my treatment process. He had my chart in his hand and repeated what I had told the nurse regarding my lump discovery. He did a breast check and told me right away that the lump was cancerous. He handed me business cards of several specialists (a surgeon, an oncologist, and a radiologist) and suggested that I make an appointment with the surgeon as soon as possible.

What! I couldn't believe what I'd just heard. I wondered, *Did the doctor just tell me I have breast cancer without giving me an X-ray, a sonogram, a PET scan, or a mammogram?* My head was spinning. I was speechless. I felt like standing in the middle of that examination room and screaming at the top of my lungs, "What is happening?" Upon hearing this diagnosis, what I needed was an empathetic doctor, one who genuinely cared about his patient. Trust me, that was not the case.

The doctor dismissed me and quickly moved on to the next patient. I was so shocked and scared in that moment that I could not even begin to ask any questions. I felt like a lost child desperately trying to find her mother. It is an understatement to say I felt alone, insecure, and confused!

CHAPTER TWO

Follow the Yellow Brick Road

The yellow brick road in *The Wizard of Oz* reminds me of my journey, of trying to find my way back to a place of comfort before being diagnosed with breast cancer and going through surgeries and treatment. And, yes, I am from Kansas and love *The Wizard of Oz*.

Like Dorothy, I faced a tornado that challenged me and tested my strength and faith. In my situation, following the yellow brick road helped me embrace my wellness and focus on healing.

My husband was just as shocked as I was about the physician's rude behavior. But Byrd is extremely positive and supportive and knew we had to move forward regardless of this negative experience. When we returned home from the appointment, I began sorting out the medical specialist cards the doctor had given me. I decided to schedule an appointment with a breast surgeon whose office was in the same professional building as my gynecologist's office. My thinking was that at least they could communicate quickly if necessary. Besides, I had very little time to research breast surgeons. So I followed the recommendation of the referring doctor in my gynecologist's absence.

The first visit with the breast surgeon was on February 14, 2008. This was a positive experience. While he wasn't warm and fuzzy, he was a sincere and caring professional who took the time to explain the procedure he would perform to identify the lump. After reviewing my mammogram results from September 2007, 2006, and 2005, he stated there appeared to be a mass in the general area that almost looked cystic. Using a sterile technique, he tried to aspirate the area, hoping to extract fluid, but he could not. The surgeon determined that the area needed to be biopsied and said that he would not be insulted if we wanted to get another opinion. He gave me a booklet on breast lumps and told me he just wanted to make sure I did not have breast cancer. I told him I would call his office if I wanted to schedule the biopsy surgery.

Quite frankly, I should have scheduled my appointment then, but I was so overwhelmed with information that I just needed to exhale. I needed a break from this whole scenario. The urgency of my situation scared me. I did not have time to research what was happening to me, but I felt I needed to because the referring doctor and breast surgeon urged me to move forward within the next few days. I was exhausted by the overload of information, and I was trying to understand that several different medical terms had the same meaning. For example, a breast conserving surgery is also known as a lumpectomy. So I needed to take a deep breath, regroup, and put everything in perspective. At this point, though, I knew I needed to move forward with the biopsy to confirm what I already knew in my heart.

Biopsy

A biopsy is performed when a suspicious breast lump is found by the patient, doctor, or imaging studies. This procedure takes a tissue sample to be examined under the microscope to see if cancer cells are present. There are several different types of breast biopsies. A biopsy may be done with a needle. The doctor removes a piece of breast tissue by inserting a needle through the skin into the breast. In a surgical biopsy, a surgeon uses a scalpel to cut through the skin and remove a larger piece of the suspicious breast tissue.

I hesitated to contact my siblings before my biopsy. I did not want them to worry at this stage of the process. Of course, that was not going to happen because my vocal, can't-keep-a-secret twin sister, Claudette, called them even before I had a chance. Except for Claudette, most of my siblings live out of town. Besides, coming from a very close-knit family, we tend not to keep critical information from each other. After Claudette let the cat out of the bag, I found myself having to manage everyone's emotions. My siblings had lots of questions and anxiety, and I sensed an edge of possible fear. I was not surprised because that is normal; asking questions and being nervous is what we do in order to understand a situation. It's all good!

On February 25, 2008, Byrd, my older twin sisters, Wanda and Paula, and my brother-in-law, Fred, waited patiently for the breast surgeon's findings after my biopsy. I recall the night before my biopsy; my family, some of whom had come from out of town to support me, was in our living room, and Byrd put a couple of logs in the fireplace. We were enjoying the fire and each other before winding down for the night. I began to feel the heavy weight of what the following day might bring. Oh, my God, I was full of anxiety and sensed the atmosphere was changing in the room.

At this point, my nerves were overpowering me. I was anxious to find out the results, and I was scared, knowing what I already knew. The laughter slowed down, and the look of worry started settling on our faces. I know my family members thought they were fine; however, I saw something different. I excused myself and went upstairs to take a hot bubble bath. Eventually, everyone went to bed because I had to be at the hospital at six o'clock am the next day. The next morning, we all appeared to be ready for whatever the results of my biopsy procedure showed.

While I was in recovery, the breast surgeon informed them that my lump was cancerous. They told me later on that my sisters cried while my husband and brother-in-law appeared to remain strong. I can only imagine their worry.

When I woke up in the recovery room, the breast surgeon told me the lump was cancerous. The nurse at my bedside offered me a Kleenex. I said, "No thank you." I did not feel like crying. At this point, the severity of my situation was not quite a reality. I felt somewhat relieved to have confirmation about what I already knew. There was no need to panic and upset my family. If I had, this whole scenario would have been different. Immediately, faith triumphed over fear because I knew I was traveling down an unfamiliar road. I knew I needed to stay strong and positive because I had no idea what was going to happen each step of the way. All I wanted was for the tumor to be removed. The breast surgeon recommended a lumpectomy.

My sisters and I had lunch in Virginia that same afternoon. While we enjoyed our outing, we were clearly uneasy. We avoided discussing my diagnosis. At first I wondered why my sisters did not bring up my biopsy results and ask me how I was feeling. I thought back to when the nurse pushed my wheelchair from the recovery room to the family waiting area; my sisters said, "You will be fine. You know we are here for you." At lunch, I could see that they, too, were trying to process my situation. I am sure they did not want to add any more anxiety to our day. We ended up having a wonderful time together in spite of it all and later went shopping with Claudette, who was making some improvements to her house. Ah, retail therapy! After shopping we went back to my house in Maryland. Although I was extremely exhausted from the day's activities, I began to acknowledge that I now fit the category of a breast cancer patient. Even though I had some discomfort from the biopsy, I was physically fine overall. While I had mixed emotions that day, I tried not to show it.

Byrd, my confidant, friend, and loving husband called several friends over that evening. He knew their presence would lift our spirits up. Their company was a general comfort to all of us. Even though I believed I showed no anxiety, Byrd wanted me to be embraced with all the love my heart could hold from the people I loved.

Byrd and I are both extroverts, and we both love people. Byrd knew that the participation of family and friends would be a critical part of my healing. And for me, this had its very own special healing powers. They promoted the love, support, inspiration, and encouragement I needed for achieving the best possible outcome throughout my wellness process. I did take notice that evening that my friends were trying their best to pretend that there was nothing wrong; they took care not to mention that coming over to my house on a weeknight was unusual for them. I know them oh so well. This was the point when I began to manage their emotions by reassuring them everything was going to be fine, especially when everyone continued to ask how I was holding up. Even though my mind kept drifting while my friends were there, I could not help but wonder what this unfamiliar process was really about. Despite my feelings, I kept my spirits up and continued to enjoy my family and friends.

Wanda notified my employer of the results of my biopsy later that afternoon and let them know I would be off for the rest of the week. She also called family members and close friends. Later that evening, my telephone rang constantly. Within days, my friends were visiting, bringing flowers, plants, angels, cards, and enough food to feed an army throughout my entire treatment. I received many inspirational gifts—books, therapy exercise regimens, fruit baskets, gift baskets, and more. Many of the rooms in my house were filled with the fragrance of flowers. I remember thinking, *Is this what will happen if I die?* My home looked like a funeral parlor. While I appreciated everyone's kindness, I was overwhelmed with the constant attention. After all, I was still trying to grasp what was to come next.

Two days after the results of my surgical biopsy, we met with my breast surgeon in his office. He expressed his sympathy about the findings of breast cancer. He noted that my previous mammogram was normal, although he was a little concerned about the area behind the areola. He thought my breast cancer may be fairly extensive and was not sure if he would be able to do breast conserving surgery, known as a lumpectomy. A lumpectomy removes only the tumor and a rim of normal surrounding breast tissue. If cancer cells are present at the margin, the outside edge of the biopsy, then more surgery would be required to remove any remaining cancer. Most often, this additional surgery is a repeat. He went over the possibility that I may need chemotherapy and radiation if I had a lumpectomy.

A mastectomy removes the entire breast. If I had a mastectomy, the surgeon explained that I may still need radiation if something was in my lymph nodes.

The surgeon went over everything thoroughly with my family and gave us the state-required booklet on breast cancer, information on sentinel node biopsies, and copies of my preliminary pathology report. Wanda was the spokesperson for our family because she was familiar with this process—several friends of hers have gone through the breast cancer journey. I was so glad my family was there because I don't remember a thing the surgeon said except, "I am sorry; the findings showed this tumor is cancerous."

How could this have happened? When Allan was born in January 1989, I underwent a complete hysterectomy and was placed on estrogen therapy. As I now understand it, the recommended time frame for taking estrogen therapy is seven years or less. Unfortunately, my first gynecologist, who initially placed me on the estrogen therapy for five years, retired. My second gynecologist continued this estrogen therapy at a lower dose for ten more years before she relocated her business to another state. My third gynecologist continued to keep me on the low dose of estrogen for three and a half years and decided to wean me off by January 2008. I discovered my lump a month later on February 8, 2008. I was later told by my breast surgeon that my cancer was estrogen-driven.

Tests

The surgeon ordered additional tests to find out if the cancer had spread and to help determine the best treatment. Over two days, I had a series of tests, including a chest X-ray, a bone scan, a CT scan, an MRI, an EKG and several blood tests, all in preparation for the upcoming lumpectomy. These tests were not painful, but after the events of the previous few days, I was further exhausted after the two days of testing. There may have been other tests, but these are the ones that I recall. I was just going through the motions. Again, thank God Claudette and Wanda accompanied me to my appointments.

After my appointments, Claudette wanted to continue her search for accessories to finish her designing project. We were traveling to Home Goods store in Crofton, Maryland when I told her start moving into the right lane for a turn she would need to make. She panicked and felt I did not give her enough time to exchange lanes, and she started arguing with me. I was calm with her and then she said in an angry voice, "You are just calm because you were told you have cancer." Wow. I did not respond. We continued down the road in silence, listening to the music. When we arrived at Home Goods store, we grabbed shopping carts and started looking for Claudette's accessories. Claudette and I ended up in the same aisle, and all of a sudden her face was red and she started crying uncontrollably and apologized. We embraced each other in the middle of the aisle while she continued to cry. She said, "Sister, I am scared!"

Her emotions made me realize that this process was not mine alone. After all, Claudette inherited my morning sickness when I was pregnant with both of my sons. Only a twin would understand this. During my process, it was crucial to include friends and family members.

Sentinel Lymph Node Mapping, Biopsy, and Lumpectomy Surgery

My breast surgeon recommended lumpectomy surgery. My husband and I understood that the goal of a lumpectomy was to try to spare and preserve as much of the breast tissue as possible.

Our physician explained to us that, before the lumpectomy took place, he would perform a sentinel lymph node mapping and biopsy. This procedure would check for the presence of cancer cells in the lymph node. A biopsy of right axillary nodes and a lumpectomy were performed on March 14, 2008, sixteen days after my initial biopsy. By then, my sisters and brother-in-law had returned to their homes in Phoenix and Chicago.

Before we left our house on the day of my surgery, I tried to tell my husband that, in case God transitions me from this earth, there are things that need to be handled. He did not want to discuss business matters or how he should embrace our sons after my death. He said, "Hon, everything is going to be fine; God did not bring you this far without a plan." Byrd was positive, confident, and scared all at the same time. My anxiety level was all over the place, and only he knew it.

Byrd, Warren, Claudette, her daughter Cimone, and my friends Marilyn, Bernetta, and Carolyn were all sitting around the family table at the hospital. We had barely sat down at the table when the nurse came for me. "It's time to get prepared for surgery," she said. Oh, no! We didn't have time to pray together. Marilyn, being a prayer warrior, asked the nurse to give us a few more minutes. I was relieved because I needed prayer to anchor me and relieve me from the anxiety. I thought about family, siblings, and friends and their possible reactions should God decided to transition me into his kingdom. Everything was happening so quickly. We prayed together. I felt so much better and was now ready to face whatever God had in store for me. I was at peace.

Around 9:20 am the day of the surgery, I was taken to a holding area where I sat in a comfortable chair. My breast surgeon injected a radioactive substance, technetium 99 sulfur colloid, into the area around the tumor near the areola and massaged it into the skin. Lymphatic vessels carried these materials to the sentinel lymph node. The surgeon then detected the radioactivity with a Geiger counter in the sentinel node. Then he cut the node out and examined it under a microscope. The final pathologic diagnosis revealed the right axillary sentinel lymph nodes #1 and #2 were positive for microscopic focus of carcinoma, an invasive form of breast cancer.

Around 11:30 am, I was taken back to the operating room and given general anesthesia. My tumor was about two inches. The surgeon wanted to ensure complete removal, so he separated the tumor into two portions. I believe my surgery lasted about three to four hours. The surgeon was pleased with how the surgery went and told me he wanted to see me within the next week for follow-up. I stayed overnight in the hospital for observation. I did not suffer pain from the surgery. Intravenous tubes remained in my arm, delivering medication. This heavy dose of morphine was probably the reason I felt no pain. I took an overdue vacation in my mind and slept the entire day with the exception of nurses checking my status. To tell you the truth, I hardly noticed them because I was truly out of it. The next day, I was released to go home. I couldn't wait to be curled up in my comfortable bed and be with my family.

I recall several cancer patients telling me that their doctors gave them a choice of having either a lumpectomy or a mastectomy. I was not offered a choice. I admit I felt disrespected and confessed, "Why didn't my surgeon ask me what I preferred?" Ultimately, I accepted and trusted my surgeon's recommendation. Most of the women I spoke with were under the impression that, by having a mastectomy, they would not have to undergo cancer treatments, such as chemotherapy and/or radiation. They also thought it might possibly limit their chances of having the cancer reoccur. I asked my breast surgeon, "Do women who have had a mastectomy versus a lumpectomy have a reduced chance of cancer recurrence?" He told me that every woman's chance of survival is different and that I should focus on my wellness. I had a moment of sheer panic, uncertain of my own cancer journey. Fear took over my faith.

My dear friend Beverly, whom I affectionately call "Bevie," contacted our friend Tanya, to see if she was available to serve as my advocate throughout the treatment process. I admit I didn't even know that the role of a breast cancer advocate existed. And honestly, this was the furthest thing from my mind at the time. Thinking about what I needed was difficult because I was unfamiliar with the treatment process. The shock of the diagnosis and trying to balance my family and work life made it all quite overwhelming, to say the least. Thankfully, Beverly had the foresight to know what I needed.

Tanya became my breast cancer advocate. Her role was to provide guidance to me and Byrd throughout the remainder of my breast cancer journey. She accompanied us to meetings to ensure that, emotions aside, we understood the steps in the process. Tanya attended almost all of my doctor appointments. I was glad Tanya came to every meeting because, quite frankly, there were times I was so fatigued that my attention span focused on crawling in my bed and sleeping this situation away. I don't know what I would have done without her by my side.

She was familiar with the treatment process, having had several family members and friends who battled the disease. Not only is Tanya an excellent communicator, but also she knew the right questions to ask my doctors and noted their responses. She was always prepared for my appointments because of the research she conducted ahead of time. The entire process was daunting, and Tanya called me regularly to ensure I clearly understood what was going on.

She joined Byrd and me for the follow-up appointment to my lumpectomy. The surgeon told us that he was assigning a more advanced stage of cancer. The stage tells how large your tumor is and how far the cancer has spread. This classification is designed to help both the patient and doctor decide what kind of treatment would be best moving forward. He explained the different stages in detail.

Stages of Breast Cancer

Stage O:

Very early breast cancer or pre-invasive cancer. This type of cancer has *not* spread within or outside of the breast (also called in situ or noninvasive cancer).

Stage I:

Tumor of two cm (one inch) or smaller. No cancer is found in the lymph nodes in the armpit or outside the breast.

Stage II:

Tumor of two cm (one inch) or smaller. Cancer is found in the lymph nodes in the armpit.
Tumor of between two and five cm (one and two inches). Cancer may or may not be found in the lymph nodes in the armpit.
Tumor of five cm (two inches) or larger. Cancer is not found in lymph nodes in the armpit.

Stage III:

Tumor of five cm (two inches) or smaller. Cancer is also in the lymph nodes that are stuck together.
Tumor of larger than five cm (two inches). Cancer is attached to other parts of the breast area, including the chest wall, ribs, and muscles.
Inflammatory breast cancer. In this rare type of cancer, the skin of the breast is red and swollen.

Stage IV:

Tumor has spread to other parts of the body, such as the bones, lungs, liver, or brain.

My pre-surgery diagnosis was stage I/II. However, the lumpectomy revealed that the tumor was in fact much deeper in the chest cavity and therefore was updated to stage III (A/B). To say that I was overwhelmed was an understatement! Tanya, Byrd, and I were shocked to hear the new diagnosis. The surgeon said that once the incision was made, he was able to identify the depth of the cancer. After the meeting, Tanya, Byrd, and I walked to our cars, still in shock. I felt sad. What does this really mean? I am almost at stage IV, which I have heard may be life threatening. I wondered if my cancer might have spread far beyond the new, advanced stage now. This was so disturbing. The surgeon did not seem worried because his personality is straightforward and matter-of-fact. At this moment, my world seemed shattered. I have never experienced the level of depression I did following my appointment that day.

Byrd suggested we take a drive over the Bay Bridge in Maryland. He knows that I enjoy the ride, looking down at the water and sailboats. In addition, the Queenstown Premium Outlets are located minutes away from the other end of the bridge. Ah, once again, retail therapy! Under normal circumstances, this would have been the answer. I could hardly breathe because I was so upset after learning that the cancer was more advanced.

We arrived at the Premium Outlets, but I was not interested in a long shopping spree. However, on the way out of a women's clothing store, of which I cannot even recall the name, I spotted a cute, multi-colored, sleeveless, airy-fabric blouse. I chose the blouse because the style and color gave me a momentary uplift. But once I was at the cash register, I could barely find my wallet in my purse because my eyes were welled up with tears. At any moment, I was going to burst out sobbing. This felt like one of the saddest days in my life. I managed to leave the store without crying and with the blouse. On the ride back across the Bay Bridge, I wanted to open the car door and take off running. I was just that overwhelmed.

When we returned home, I went into our sunroom, which I refer to as our "happy healing room." This room has lots of green plants and plenty of windows, allowing the sun's bright, warm rays to shine through. The room makes us feel good. Byrd asked if I wanted his company in the sunroom. I replied "no" because he had to work that evening and only had a few hours left to rest before heading out the door. I knew he was being strong for me, holding on the best way he knew how. I could see so much fear in his eyes that I could have broken down and cried. I was barely holding on, trying to be strong for both of us. Once I was alone and began to relax, I was numb. I was in a space in which fear could have been an option. Certainly, this warranted a total meltdown. I called my siblings to give them the update. They were perplexed. Even though they tried to remain calm and strong for me, I knew they were shaken to the core. This is why being strong is sometimes painful. For the life of me, I should have cried. But I thought crying would cloud my management of this process. Certainly, additional anxieties would not be helpful. Wow, was I wrong. I realized after my treatment process was complete and I began to write this book that crying was necessary for me to cleanse my mind, body, and soul. The power of healing through my tears allowed me to share my experience with you.

Byrd reluctantly went to work even though he knew my girlfriend Carolyn was coming over to sit with me for a while. He knew I was shaken to the core by the new diagnosis. I shared my update with Carolyn. She provided so much comfort and support.

About an hour into Carolyn's visit the telephone rang. My gynecologist greeted me and asked how I was doing. She received the reports from the surgeon and called to follow up. I had been upset with her for not being available during the initial days of my ordeal. She had been out of town then, and I hadn't heard from her when I had the biopsy or lumpectomy. Because of the relationship we had built up over the years, I really missed her not being there to help me navigate the cancer process. She expressed how sorry she was to hear of my news and suggested that I call her anytime I needed to talk. I believe that was the last time I ever spoke with her because I was focusing on selecting an oncologist.

My breast surgeon recommended an oncologist for follow-up treatment. However, if I wanted to locate one on my own, I had between four and six weeks to make a selection. I decided to seek a second opinion from another breast surgeon before starting chemotherapy treatment.

Axillary Lymph Node Dissection Surgery

I had a window of opportunity to research other breast surgeons for second opinions and follow-up before I began my chemotherapy treatment. I specifically requested an appointment with a female breast surgeon at MedStar Georgetown University Hospital. You can't imagine how good it felt to work with a female physician who finally understood my concerns and showed compassion. I longed for a nurturing and compassionate doctor and found it in this person. She ordered a series of tests, including a CT scan, an MRI test, and lab work.

The results revealed that, upon subsequent IHC staining (a special staining process performed on fresh or frozen breast cancer tissue removed during biopsy), additional nodes were now reading positive.

On April 10, 2008, I underwent axillary lymph node dissection surgery at MedStar Georgetown University Hospital. This procedure involves the removal and examination of the lymph nodes in the armpit to determine if breast cancer has spread to them. One lymph node was found cancerous, and an additional eleven lymph nodes were removed to ensure that the cancer did not spread beyond the initial one.

Claudette and Cimone brought me home from MedStar Georgetown University Hospital following the sentinel lymph node dissection procedure. I was given medication before the anesthesia because I have always had a difficult time with nausea under sedation. After spending a bit more time in the recovery room than the nurses anticipated, I was released to the care of my sister. I still felt nauseated even after the extra pill the nurse gave me prior to checking out.

Driving down L Street, NW, in Washington, I asked Claudette to please pull over because I had to clear my stomach. I felt like I had motion sickness, similar to what one would experience on a cruise only there was no water, and the cruise ship never left the dock. Claudette pulled over, and I darted into the alley a few feet from the car parked at the curb. Claudette followed and was trying to comfort me when, all of a sudden, a drunken man appeared. He was thin and about six feet tall. He had a gray beard, and his eyes appeared to be slightly yellowish. His clothes were dirty, and he had a brown paper bag in his hand; I am certain that inside was his favorite beverage, if you get my drift. I could smell him as he moved closer to us. He was about three feet away from Claudette and me in the alley when he started laughing loudly as if my vomiting in the trash can was the highlight of his day. He lifted his leg slightly and slapped his hand on his thigh, laughing uncontrollably. He could hardly say the words, but finally managed to blurt out, "Damn baby, you're my kind of girl, 'cause you sure know how to party!" He repeated, "Yes, indeed," over and over as he staggered down the street.

Claudette and I looked at each other and started laughing so hard that tears began to flow from our eyes. I had stopped vomiting and pulled myself together. We laughed all the way home. I thought to myself, "If he only knew I was battling cancer." Little did the drunken man know that his reaction to my hangover-like behavior (*sans* the party) lifted my spirits that day. I thank you, mystery man, for keeping it real. In my moment of struggle, you helped ease my pain. See, we all serve a purpose in life. I hope he is blessed.

After the surgery, I experienced diminished sensation at the surgical site. My right arm felt numb and sometimes tingly; it felt very tight when I attempted to stretch it over my head. The breast surgeon explained that this is usually a temporary condition and should improve with treatment. She then wrote an order for me to begin lymphedema treatment.

Lymphedema Treatment and Management

Lymphedema treatment and management aims to reduce swelling, relieve discomfort, and prevent the buildup of fluid within the body. Lymphedema, or arm swelling, is the result of localized fluid retention and swelling that is generally caused by an interruption of the lymphatic system, most commonly attributed to the surgical removal of lymph nodes. The lymphatic system is made up of lymph nodes throughout the body, which are connected by a network of lymph vessels. The lymphatic system acts as a one-way drainage system transporting extra fluid from body tissue into the blood circulation and, ultimately, out of the body. If lymph nodes or vessels become blocked, the lymph fluid is unable to pass through them. The extra fluid cannot drain away normally, thus it builds up and causes swelling. The incidence of upper-extremity lymphedema varies in women with breast cancer who have been treated with surgery, radiation or both.

I underwent lymphedema treatment and management with a physical therapist twice a week for six weeks at Doctors Community Hospital Rehabilitation Services. My physical therapist, Melissa, is intelligent, warm, funny and very passionate about her work. Her constant encouragement helped me through times when I felt too fatigued to continue.

Melissa taught me lymphedema treatment and management and made sure I felt comfortable with the process, because it would require a lot of work. Melissa explained the different ways of treating my condition.

She said the most effective method involved a combination of treatments that included the following:

- Skin care to prevent injury and infection
- Positioning and moving the limb to help drain fluid
- Compressing the limb using compression garments such as sleeves or bandages
- Exercising to improve flow of lymph fluid
- Specialized massage, called manual lymphatic drainage (MLD) or self-massage, to help shift fluid that has built up
- Deep breathing exercises

Melissa made sure I had a solid understanding of how to perform each of the treatments, but our sessions mainly focused on the MLD treatment. She relied on me to follow the prescribed treatment program on my own at home. Following therapy sessions, I wore a compression sleeve during the day and wrapped my arm in ACE bandages at night. Once I progressed to the point that the fluid level was manageable, I only wore the compression sleeve during the day.

Melissa never missed a beat. She could always tell when I did not continue the treatments at home because of the fluid buildup in my right arm and breast. With her highly skilled, gentle-yet-firm therapeutic touch, she would work me twice as hard to move the fluid along. This was a constant reminder for me to stay on top of my home lymphedema management, especially if I did not want Melissa to give me a heavy work-over. Melissa is the best!

In addition to the physical treatments, exercise and skin and limb care became an integral part of my daily life as well. The gentle exercises kept my arm and shoulder working normally. Melissa explained that patients with lymphedema must ensure that the affected area is kept clean and dry, free of bruises, cuts, sunburn, insect bites, and pet scratches, and treated specially to take precautions when flying. In addition, patients managing lymphedema should never have blood drawn from the affected limb or wear tight jewelry or elastics around the affected limb.

Although having lymphedema meant making these minor lifestyle changes, it was a manageable condition. I had to repeat this lymphedema process two months after my initial axillary lymph node dissection surgery. I had a minor surgery to remove a lump under the skin on my right arm—the same side as my tumor. My surgeon wanted to make sure that extra fluid did not build up in my arm or breast and cause swelling in those areas. Once my lymphedema was controlled, I was ready to start my chemotherapy treatments.

Chemotherapy

According to Wikipedia chemotherapy is the treatment of disease through the use of chemicals that have a specific toxic effect upon the disease-producing microorganisms or that selectively destroy cancerous tissue.

What the dictionary doesn't say is that chemotherapy requires an abundance of strength and faith on the part of the patient and his or her support system. And critical to the success of the treatment process is a skilled team of caregivers to guide and support you through it.

After endless research, I selected an oncologist at MedStar Georgetown University Hospital who came highly recommended by several people I know whose lives have been touched by cancer. I was thrilled that the oncologist I selected was an all-around good fit for me. We have a great relationship to this date. I was blessed. Quite frankly, my whole team of doctors at the hospital became like family to me. I was very confident and comfortable with them and the hospital's facilities.

The initial meeting with the oncologist was to discuss my situation and determine the best treatment plan moving forward. To prepare for the meeting with the oncologist, Byrd and I spoke with Tanya regarding the kind of questions we needed to ask.

The oncologist also spoke with me about participating in a clinical trial study. She explained the purpose of the study was to determine a medication by the name of bevacizumab (the common name for the commercial drug Avastin), in combination with other cancer-reducing medicines, reduces the risk of recurrence (termed "disease-free survival") compared to standard chemotherapy alone. On my own, I read more information about this clinical study and gave it much thought over a long weekend. Ultimately, I decided to participate in the clinical study because I wanted the best possible outcome in my wellness journey.

For my participation in the clinical trial research study, I was granted a private room for my chemotherapy sessions. The room had a wonderful outside view, cable television, a private bathroom, and access to a kitchen. Lunch was offered to me and my guest each time I came in for treatment. Most of the time, I would decline the offer because my girlfriend and I would choose a restaurant to visit for lunch following each session.

My oncologist ordered a battery of exams, tests, and procedures to determine my eligibility to participate in the study. Most of these exams, tests, and procedures were part of my regular cancer care. They included the history and physical examination, height and weight measurements, overall assessment of the impact of my breast cancer, lab testing of blood and urine, chest X-ray and CT scan of my chest, EKG, and Echocardiogram and MUGA scans. The test results proved I was eligible for participation in the clinical trial study.

To prepare for chemotherapy and the clinical trial, the surgeon implanted a mediport commonly referred to as a port. The device is implanted under the skin, usually in the upper chest, just below the collarbone. It provides access to a vein, through which chemotherapy medications are administered. While intended for temporary use during medical treatment, the mediport can remain in place permanently if necessary. When not in use, the only care a port requires is flushing once a month with heparinized saline, which keeps blood clots from forming in the line. A portion of the device, called the reservoir, can be felt just under the skin's surface. When the port is "accessed," a special needle is placed through the skin into the reservoir through a plastic membrane called a septum. A catheter under the skin connects the reservoir to a large vein, usually in the neck. This device allows the patient to have lab samples taken and to receive medication, blood, or nutrition.

My mediport was removed before I started my radiation session. I did keloid, which left a scar where the mediport was removed. For the longest time, I experienced continuous itching. To date, it feels a little tender and itches, but not for long. This scar will be a constant reminder of how blessed I was to make it through the chemotherapy part of my journey.

I received the chemotherapy drugs doxorubicin and cyclophosphamide, followed by paclitaxel with bevacizumab or a placebo, administered through my mediport. At the end of the trial study, it was revealed that I was taking bevacizumab, not a placebo. Toward the middle of my chemotherapy sessions, I had been pretty sure I was taking bevacizumab. I remember one afternoon, my nose and gums starting bleeding. At the same time, I experienced diarrhea and vomiting. I did not know where to begin to control this situation.

I frantically called out, "Byrd!" He was relaxing in our sunroom, and I know he thought I was resting upstairs in our bed. He quickly cut through our den, then down a short hall, and immediately ran into the bathroom. He started settling me down with his calm voice. He managed my situation with ease and cleaned up the mess. This helpless feeling totally exhausted all my energy for that particular day. After my husband cleaned me up, off to bed I went, sleeping the whole afternoon away. I hope never to experience this frightening situation again, even though the advantage of taking this drug resulted in a positive outcome.

Before any chemotherapy drugs were administered, I was given appropriate pre-medications to limit nausea and other potential side effects. I remember a couple of sessions when I was nauseated and vomited. Now that I think about it, I probably did not eat breakfast to settle the medication. I had lost my appetite at that time. I completed four three-week (Q3) cycles of doxorubicin/cyclophosphamide and bevacizumab and twelve weeks of weekly paclitaxel and three weeks of bevacizumab. I received six weekly infusions of paclitaxel before needing a two-week treatment break for grade three peripheral neuropathy; my treatment resumed with a 20 percent dose reduction, and I was able to complete the twelve infusions as planned. The total duration of chemotherapy was twenty-four weeks.

Once the chemotherapy regimen was established, my girlfriends encouraged me to e-mail my schedule because they wanted to participate in this process. Byrd accompanied me to my initial and final chemotherapy treatments. He encouraged me to spend the remaining sessions with my girlfriends as well because he knew it was important that they be a part of my process. Support from Pam, Terri, Bernetta, Louise, Pat, Claudette, Tanya, and Carolyn was exactly what I needed. The sessions were also an opportunity for them to share what was happing in their lives.

I sat in a teal blue, leather, very comfortable recliner chair to receive my chemotherapy drug. It was so relaxing, and besides I had offered my girlfriends the bed, which they gladly accepted. They hopped up in the bed next to my recliner with their laptops, cell phones, and magazines. Even though they took the time off from work, you and I both know how that goes. Usually, they ended up going to sleep at some point, and at times, I would drift into a really relaxed mode. At the most, my chemotherapy sessions lasted about four hours each. If I needed a blood infusion, of which I received only two, I believe we were there about five or six hours. We didn't mind because the point was spending time with each other.

At that time, the environment was abuzz with the 2008 presidential campaign. During treatments, we had lengthy, occasionally emotionally charged, discussions about what was taking place during this truly exciting time in American history. I called it "emotional therapy."

Byrd completely understood that my girlfriends were a part of the process and didn't mind giving up that time with me. He was very grateful for my friends' support and love. Their presence alone was uplifting and helped me heal more than they could possibly know. I hope somehow I was able to comfort them as well.

I underwent two blood infusions because my blood counts were down, causing me to feel fatigued. Having blood infusions is not unusual for some women going through chemotherapy. There were times it took everything I had to get out of bed. This kind of fatigue was far different than any I had ever experienced. I did not always have the will to eat, drink, or really rest well.

Sometimes trying to sit up or get out of bed took hours to accomplish. Toward the end of my chemotherapy completion, the accumulation of the heavy doses of medication continued to make me extremely fatigued. One day it took me nearly four hours to get out of bed. At times, it was more like fighting for my will to live. I began to understand why some people discontinue their treatment process.

This was a rough patch for me. I wondered when this phase was going to end, because I really had forgotten what it was to feel good. But I dealt with feeling so fatigued for many months, and I somehow accepted that this was my way of life. I persevered because I knew that it would take patience and endurance to achieve full healing. I realized I was blessed to have great energy before my journey and to have this altered through my wellness was a humbling experience. I will never take what God has given me for granted.

Side Effects of Chemotherapy

When my first and second doses of chemotherapy were administered, I felt fine. There were no negative side effects. It wasn't until the third cycle of chemotherapy that I had chills and felt a slight fever. I often wore skullcaps and wrapped myself in blankets to keep warm. I had bottles of Tums, ginger pills, and anything else that would ease the burning sensation in my stomach. There were times when my indigestion was so severe that I would ball up in a knot. This felt like I had swallowed a ball of fire and could not put out the fire. Sometimes the pain was so strong that I was too exhausted for tears.

It took weeks for this to go away. I stopped wishing every day to feel better because it seemed to make this healing process longer. Without placing a rush order to God to speed up my healing, I knew that, in due time, eventually everything would be all right. By keeping my faith, I learned patience.

For a while, I had loss of appetite and experienced nausea, vomiting, and diarrhea. I lost quite a bit of weight in a relatively short period of time. My oncologist recommended that I eat ice cream, malts, and milk shakes for extra calories because losing weight was not an option while going through my treatment. Popsicles were my favorite because they soothed the soreness in my throat and deflated my swollen tongue. My girlfriend Pat always kept the popsicles coming. This was a treat.

Twice a day, my neighbor Bernetta would come to my house to prepare healthy beverages: a fruit drink in the morning before she went to work and a veggie drink in the evening. I didn't like the veggie drink at all, but Bernetta encouraged me to drink it to maintain my strength.

Also, before some of my chemotherapy treatments, my co-worker and friend, Lane, who I affectionately call "Lydia," would prepare chemo meals for me. The meals would include soup and homemade bread. Lane also added other foods and treats to complete her meal packages. Lane was so kind and supportive. She understood what this breast cancer journey was about because she is close to several people who were diagnosed with some form of cancer.

My body retained fluid throughout this entire process. To date, I have to make a conscious effort to balance my weight through nutrition and regular exercise. I am not quite there, but I will never give up on trying to maintain a healthier life style.

After that third session of chemotherapy, my hair follicles started to loosen. When my hair began to shed, I decided to cut it very short. Soon it began falling out in patches until, ultimately, my husband's barber, Chris, cut off all my hair and shaved my head. Cutting my hair and shaving my head was the most liberating feeling I have ever known. There was no place to hide because I was totally exposed. I wore my bald head with complete pride and confidence. This was the only time I had control of the change in my treatment process. Before I shaved my head, I never really gave myself full permission to be me. What an awesome feeling to see who you really are through change in your life. Beauty does start from within.

My hands and fingernails soon began to change in color to a dark gray/black, which took months to return to normal. The chemotherapy drugs also damaged the nerve endings in my hands and feet. This is called peripheral neuropathy, which causes numbness and/or tingling, burning or freezing pain, or a prickling sensation.

It's funny that I only remember the discussions about my chemotherapy treatment plan and not the side effects, such as peripheral neuropathy. After the third cycle of chemotherapy, I started feeling the symptoms of peripheral neuropathy. To date, there are days I have to ease out of bed by carefully and softly placing my feet on the floor. Most of the time, my feet are tight at the balls of my feet and around the ankles. At times, I flex my ankles and feet just to feel some relief. I walk as often as possible because this does help somewhat. One thing is for sure—when it rains, I can feel the pain running through my body and settling in my feet.

This condition has left me clumsy at times. I can't be trusted to hold something in my hands for longer than a minute because, all of a sudden, the object I'm holding can gently slip from my hands without any warning. I have undergone physical therapy, including water exercises, twice. While it temporarily ease the pain for the moment, only time will tell if the pain will ever go away completely.

In the beginning, I struggled with accepting that I now am or can be a clumsy person, especially when this was not true before. For now, a high-heeled shoe would not work. If I am wearing a low heel or a flat, enclosed shoe, at least my shoes would remain on my feet should I stumble. Trust me, I learned from past experiences.

Most of the time, I am on the move and don't always feel the pain. When I lay down at night, my pain is the worst. I have learned to manage my pain by exercising, drinking lots of water, getting my feet massaged regularly by my husband, and taking an over-the-counter pain pill every now and then. As of the writing of this book, my peripheral neuropathy is severe. I have learned to live with this condition daily.

Here's the good news; at the end of the day, I know I am blessed to be alive.

Following my final chemotherapy treatment in November 2008, when I officially learned that I had been receiving the drug bevacizumab and not a placebo, I was relieved. What a blessing to have the promise of a more effective treatment while going through this process.

I was also blessed and grateful to have formed wonderful relationships with the MedStar Georgetown University Hospital staff. They were so professional, warm, and caring. I will always cherish positive memories of how well the staff took care of me. In fact, once my chemotherapy sessions ended, I felt a bit of sadness about no longer seeing the staff whom I had grown to love and appreciate. To tell the truth, the staff spoiled me and, yes, I admit I looked forward to this special treatment every time I went to chemotherapy sessions.

Chemotherapy treatments ended a few days before Thanksgiving.

Radiation Therapy

I was absolutely exhausted after I completed the chemotherapy treatments. I was dealing with all the side effects of these drugs, but the extreme fatigue was the most pronounced. I was not looking forward to radiation because I was tired of everything that I had experienced in the last nine months. I was exhausted just thinking about all I had gone through: the biopsy procedure, the sentinel lymph node mapping and biopsy, the lumpectomy surgery, the axillary lymph node dissection surgery, the lymphedema treatment and management therapy (twice), the chemotherapy drugs, the clinical trial drug, the two blood infusions, various medications and blood drawings, many doctor appointments, and test after test after test. All I wanted was a month to recover. Oh well, life goes on, and I was glad to be alive.

I began radiation treatments the last week of December 2008 and ended January 29, 2009. I underwent forty-eight sessions of radiation in total.

The radiation process was sometimes long and painful. I felt fatigued, anxious, depressed, frustrated, and alone. I remember experiencing one side effect in particular; the external beam of radiation caused severe burns at the focal point of the beam, resulting in the peeling of the skin on my breast. My right breast was so raw from the burn that it looked pink. I was prescribed a soothing cream to help heal and moisturize the affected area. In the meantime, I could not wear a bra or a fitted blouse unless it was 100 percent cotton, because anything else might have caused infection. The healing process for the burns seemed to take forever.

It took up to six months after radiation therapy was over to gain back my much-needed, much-longed-for energy. Once the radiation treatments were completed, I was placed on a daily tamoxifen citrate twenty mg tablet for two years. Now, I am finished with the tamoxifen citrate and I have been placed on the exemestane twenty-five mg tablet daily. These pills help maintain my health status. While I feel my weight has increased due to these pills, I have learned that a balance of nutrition and exercise can help me maintain a healthier lifestyle. I thank God for giving me the strength to successfully complete this final treatment process.

Each person's surgeries, treatment plan, and side effects are different. The key is to select a team of medical professionals whom you trust and feel comfortable with. This made it easy for me to embrace each step of my process. I was open to learn, so I could better understand the process, regardless of whether or not it was associated with pain. I believe when you embrace your journey, healing will empower you to advance positively to the next step in your future.

I forgot to cry because going through the motions took precedence over my emotions. Somehow I believed that not getting emotional would allow me to stay focused on completing my surgeries and treatments without additional stress and anxiety. I had no time for a pity party, especially without the guest list.

My journey has taught me that I was wrong; if I had released my tears, I would have felt much better. My pastor once said in a sermon, "When you conceal, you cannot heal." I took this message to heart. What I have come to appreciate is that letting go of your emotions, whether you are by yourself or with another person, is an inexpensive therapy.

CHAPTER THREE

Byrd and the Boys

Part of moving through a successful treatment was making sure that my family and I were on the same page. They needed to understand the changes in my process and know what support to offer. It was important for me that my husband and two sons understood the importance of embracing our journey, particularly if we were to learn and grow from this experience.

At times, it was difficult to keep our sons updated on what was going on with me. Therefore, my husband and I decided we would share only crucial information. While I always have good conversations with our sons, I wanted to make sure I understood what they were feeling. Most of the time, our sons would say, "Mom, I am okay; you just get well." After my treatments were completed, I decided to ask my sons if they would share their feelings and thoughts about this. I knew they would be more agreeable now that my pain and suffering was at a minimum. I was glad that my family members were open to share their feelings because this meant we all were beginning to heal.

Byrd has been my friend and confidante for more than thirty-four years. I said to Byrd, "I am glad the treatment phase of this process is finally over." By February 2009, my doctors' appointments were not as frequent. My appointments were now every three months.

As I began to feel better, Byrd suggested that we take a late summer trip to the Outer Banks in North Carolina, one of our favorite vacation spots. While there, I made the decision to write this book. The Outer Banks is very peaceful place, relaxing and fun. Watching the seagulls, listening to the strong waves, collecting seashells, and walking barefoot on the beach bring me great comfort. I love it there. I can hear myself think. The Outer Banks getaway was long overdue; it was very liberating, healing, and inspiring to be there because I couldn't remember the last time I had been alone.

Throughout my cancer journey, well-meaning family and friends were always available to comfort me and lift my spirits. While they were great medicine, I definitely looked forward to some time alone with my thoughts. I would awaken early each morning and venture down to the beach, hoping to catch the sunrise as I recorded my breast cancer journey on a little Sony cassette machine. This time was most healing, and it provided the calm I needed to recall and record my experience as a breast cancer survivor.

Byrd was so excited about my decision to write a book to inspire others facing breast cancer that he also wanted to share his journey as a spouse going through the wellness process. I was more than excited about his willingness to share his feelings. I decided to interview everyone involved to understand and include his or her personal experience during my cancer journey. It was well over five months before Byrd was ready to respond. I found myself getting very frustrated with him because I felt he was making excuses for not doing his part. I also felt that Warren and Allan dodged my attempts to schedule interview time. I was hurt and felt they were being selfish. It was very painful for me to ask them to revisit this time of uncertainty in our lives; when they didn't comply with my request, I felt the pain even deeper.

At this point, I was still dealing with neuropathy. Every day presented a challenge to find ways to manage the discomfort and pain. I wanted so desperately to take a detour from the pain and focus on writing.

I shared my frustrations about Byrd's quietness with my girlfriend Pat. She knew that I was using a tape recorder to capture my story because the neuropathy often prevented me from physically writing or typing. She said, "To encourage Byrd to get started with his thoughts, offer him a tape recorder; that way, he can record his thoughts when he's ready to share about this hugely emotional experience."

It was January 2010, and Byrd still had not recorded his responses about his experience during my wellness journey. Byrd finally came around two weeks later; he was ready to be interviewed, as opposed to freely recording his own thoughts. At this point, however, I was reluctant about revisiting that painful time during my treatments. I was now at a place where most of my physical pain was beginning to subside. Emotionally, I was already moving forward with the new chapter in my life. I was physically and emotionally beginning to heal. I was not interested in going back down "Cancer Lane," even though I knew that doing so would bring closure and promote further healing. In the end, I was glad I moved forward with interviewing Byrd because it proved to be a true healing experience for the both of us.

At one point, I felt that my family members and friends were avoiding me, just like Byrd and our sons. They said, "Let me get back with you next week," or "I will give you a call when I have an available moment." Months had gone by and still no one had committed to an interview time. What I realized was that my family and friends needed their own healing space; and they needed it to be on their terms, not mine. Their reactions clearly confirmed that my breast cancer journey was about us and not me alone. Everyone was a part of my process, and we all needed healing from what we had experienced.

Timing proved to be everything. During back-to-back snowstorms in January and February 2010, most establishments in the Washington, DC, metropolitan area were closed. This was the blessing that allowed me to reflect and capture most of my interviews over the phone from family and friends. I created a set of questions and audiotaped everyone's responses. It's funny; when I initially wanted everyone's response to my interview questions, I wasn't prepared for how I would deliver those questions without revealing my pain. I could only imagine how difficult and awkward this might have been for all of us. Timing is everything without a doubt. Thank you, Lord, because I believe true healing began for all of us during those snowstorms. The word freedom comes to mind, which is ironic because we were all trapped in our houses due to the snow!

I was thrilled because I felt now I could continue to write about my journey. We all were able to let go and express our real feelings. I was so inspired about the progress I made in moving forward with my book that I started writing while listening to music. Even though I didn't write to music all the time, whenever my spirit led me in that direction it felt good. Ah, there is nothing like music therapy.

During my conversation with Byrd, he shared his initial reaction to my telephone call at 2:45 am the morning I discovered a lump in my right breast. While he was worried, he said "Hun, everything will be all right; we must continue to keep the faith." Because Byrd is a man of great faith and knew my strength, he said, "I did not feel your situation was associated with death." Byrd stated that, within his heart, he knew I would manage the treatment process because I was positive and strong, even though none of us knew then what I would be facing.

Byrd's real concern was how I was handling everything. For the most part, I remained rather calm throughout my entire process. My goal was to get through it with the best possible outcome. After discovering the lump, neither one of us accepted the potential severity of my situation. I believe this is when denial came into play. I must say, though, that our denial was based more on our faith. Even though our faith was strong, we had never faced a family situation like this before.

Byrd was very concerned about my thoughts and feelings in the early days, but he never expressed how he was truly feeling. I asked why he didn't just ask me. He said, "I felt that asking would create additional anxiety for you , so I just kept a watchful eye." Byrd knew that eventually we would talk about how we both were feeling.

I asked Byrd what his thoughts were about the doctor's diagnosis. Though he understood how stressful it was for me to receive the news, especially from a doctor I'd never met before, he said he was relieved to know what we were dealing with.

Curious, I asked Byrd for his observation of me when I first shared the doctor's diagnosis with him. He said that, having been with me for more than thirty years, he knew me quite well, and his first observation of me, as in many other situations, was that I was calm and didn't appear too distressed. He knew I was being strong, and this put him at ease.

Byrd was right on point about not seeing any distress in me at that point. There was no time for me to cry or fall apart, because I needed to be strong for you, the boys, our family and friends. My nature has always been to make people feel comfortable. This situation was no exception. I needed everyone to be positive as I began to understand and go through my process. I was desperately grasping for balance in my family life and work life. I forgot to cry because I was so overwhelmed. Only sleep could erase my anxiety.

Byrd was very anxious because he wanted the lump in my right breast removed immediately, especially since we didn't know how long it had been growing in my body. When my twin sisters and brother-in-law flew in from Phoenix and Chicago, I noticed that Byrd seemed to distance himself. He said, "I wanted to give your family their space and time alone with you." But I don't think it was my family members who needed their space; I think it was Byrd. Byrd grew up as an only child and, although he loves being around people, he is accustomed to quiet and being alone when it comes to dealing with serious circumstances in life. On the other hand, my sisters and brother-in-law are very outgoing people and would have liked nothing more than to be in Byrd's company. They understand him, though, and love him unconditionally.

Once the breast surgeon confirmed my diagnosis, Byrd felt a sense of relief, even though the lump was cancerous. "Just learning of the next steps toward getting you well felt like a burden lifted," he said. I'll never forget how Byrd surprised me by inviting a few close friends over to lift my spirits and visit with my family. Byrd's timing has always been on point, especially when he surprises me. Yep, that's my husband!

Byrd's two main concerns were that my tumor be completely removed and that I not struggle coming out of the anesthesia. In the past, I had problems handling anesthesia. Byrd said, "I felt a strong sense of relief once the lumpectomy surgery was completed and the breast surgeon said everything went well."

He added, "The most painful time for me was watching you suffer from the chemotherapy and radiation treatments." It was difficult for him to see me dealing with nausea, vomiting, light headedness, chills, fatigue, nose bleeds, decreased appetite, peripheral neuropathy, digestive problems, hair loss, weight balance, darkening of my hands and feet, and a persistent feeling of weakness.

Byrd said, "I endured your pain from the time I woke up until bedtime, but clearly not in the way you did." It broke his heart to watch me suffer, but he was inspired by my positive disposition.

Byrd wished that Claudette could have spent as much time with me as my other friends did throughout my treatment process. Claudette is a single mother who has a busy life. She did accompany me to the surgeries and a chemotherapy treatment, and she called and visited as often as she could. I understood then, as I do now, that life goes on, but there is nothing like a sister's love and comfort to make you feel safe. Much love to you, Claudette, for being the other half of my life.

Byrd said, "My role was being the best caretaker I could be, making sure you had everything you needed, holding you at night, massaging your feet, and rubbing your head and hands." Byrd always believed, since day one in our marriage, that there is nothing like the human touch, especially for purposes of healing. He was so right. He was and is my therapy.

One particular time, Byrd looked extremely worried. Usually, he is a calm, mild-mannered man, but when the breast surgeon told us that my cancer had advanced from stage I to stage III (and not understanding exactly what that meant), we both became very disturbed. Byrd quickly avoided speaking about the updated diagnosis, stating that doctors are not God. Still, at the moment the breast surgeon disclosed that my cancer had advanced, I observed that my husband seemed to age ten years. He didn't have to admit to me how he was feeling; I saw it on his face. Nonverbal reactions can reveal one's deepest emotion.

Byrd said with great conviction and sincerity, "I was feeling your pain throughout your entire process. Each day you suffered, I did too. To see you so weak at times, it broke my heart. I kept the faith and knew you would come back strong one day." Byrd's commitment to our love and my wellness gave me the strength to heal quicker than he knows. I love him!

Byrd believes that people who serve as a caretaker for someone going through a health crisis and wellness journey may experience all or some of the seven stages of grief. Those seven stages include shock and disbelief, denial and isolation, anger, bargaining, guilt, depression, and acceptance. These stages are relevant when dealing with an unexpected critical illness or other wellness circumstances.

Byrd experienced the first stage, shock and disbelief, when I first discovered my lump. He did not become angry, but at times he felt depressed and helpless during my surgeries and treatments. Even though he accepted my situation early in the process, it did not ease the pain of watching me become weak. Byrd said, "I felt it was important to let go and grieve, even if it was in private. Keeping the faith, being positive, and embracing the changes that came with these circumstances helped us grow." We survived the storm. After going through the stages of grief, I have to admit that, regardless of the pain and suffering, our lives are richer having experienced the breast cancer journey together.

My biggest concern was when to share my diagnosis with our youngest son. Allan was a freshman attending college in Virginia, about four hours from home. After socializing, partying, and adjusting to campus life, he eventually settled down and focused on his studies. I did not want to tell Allan when I first discovered my lump because he was in the midst of final exams. Four days before my family arrived from out of town, I shared my diagnosis with Allan.

Allan was able to come home three days before my biopsy. He caught a ride with a friend from campus, who was also from Maryland and whose mother was also battling breast cancer. I am glad Allan was able to visit with his aunts and uncle, who had just arrived too. His visit was short, but I was so glad to have him near me. Allan returned to school Sunday afternoon before the biopsy. Allan knew I would share the outcome of my procedure with him as soon as possible. I could sense he was deeply concerned but comforted by my strength.

Allan was twenty-one when I interviewed him about his experience. He was in total disbelief when he first learned of my breast cancer diagnosis. "God, not my mom," he said. He had great difficulty accepting my situation, watching me grow weak and fatigued after my surgeries and treatments, and dealing with all that the healing process entailed. He did not like my bald head.

One day, Allan pointed out that I had lost my eyebrows, eyelashes, and facial hair. I had been thinking, weeks before he pointed this out, why all of a sudden I began to look different. Allan was right; I had no hair. Without any hair on my whole head (hair, brows, or lashes), I thought I resembled an alien from Mars. Allan knew that humor was one of my requirements for healing throughout my wellness process. His loving nature and fun personality sparked our hearty laughs time and time again. I laughed at myself in order to get through the pain.

At first I wasn't doing so well accepting the frequent physical changes, but eventually I gave myself permission to look ugly in my eyes. So often women feel we must always look good. I ultimately stopped being hard on myself about my physical changes. Truthfully, I became determined to feel comfortable while embracing this journey for the long run.

It took Allan a while to accept that his mom would continue to experience changes. Allan was full of anxiety. He said, "At first, I thought the worst because I associated cancer with death. I did not want to lose my mom." He told me every morning was challenging for him because he knew I was suffering and could do nothing about it.

Allan said, "After settling down from the initial shock, I felt God would not take you away from me. But I wanted God to stop your pain." I later told Allan that God did answer his prayers because I began to regain my strength slowly but surely. Allan teased me and said, "God gave you a makeover, Mom." Allan was so right about that, far more than he could ever imagine.

Allan is the apple of my eye. I hope he always remembers to live his life to the fullest and keep his eyes on the prize. My philosophy is that without the test, there is no testimony. Both our sons understand that we grow from lessons learned.

Warren Jerome was twenty-eight at the time of his interview. He is a kind, loving, sensitive, good-natured person who is very supportive of his family and friends. Warren was afraid when I discovered my lump. We had a very long conversation that night about . . . oh, about everything. He said, "Mom, we can beat this. Our family will step up to the plate even more and be there for you to ensure your wellness journey is as comfortable as possible."

Warren observed that it is always a challenge when one is used to a routine, and then suddenly, a family member is faced with an issue that requires change for everyone. He said you have to adapt to a different process. He believed that God would not give us any more than we could handle.

I asked Warren if he was he afraid to share his feelings with me regarding my situation. He said, "No, because each person handles his or her situation according to what he or she can manage. Mom, I know I can talk to you anytime, and I also know you will openly share your feelings as well."

Warren shared that my diagnosis and journey had an impact on his own life and that unexpected situations are a reality; he will not take life for granted at my age. He said, "If for some reason, God did transition you to another life, I needed to be more stable because dad, my brother, and I would have to continue on our own." This was definitely the time for Warren to further develop as a man.

Warren is also the apple of my eye. In a lot of ways, he and I are alike. I am proud of my son! I hope he keeps learning and growing and becoming a leader by using his gifts to bless someone else. My message to you, Warren: Never give up because your gifts can make a difference in other people's lives.

What I learned through interviewing my family, siblings, and friends was that this was the toughest part of my healing process. It broke my heart to ask everyone to revisit this time of uncertainty in our lives. I believe the sheer weight of the unknown took a toll on all of us in some way. And even though all of them appeared strong throughout my entire process, I recognized their pain and worry, and I felt sad and guilty that my situation caused additional anxiety in their lives. I felt this way even though I knew I had little control over my situation. I came to realization that the beauty of situations like this is that love that binds us to each other and to God.

CHAPTER FOUR

Healing with Acts of Love and Support

This chapter is about the kind acts of friends who kept my spirits uplifted. Their thoughtfulness was the healing dose we all needed. I remember Marilyn, my dear friend, arranged a celebration at Ruth's Chris Steak House for my one-year anniversary as a breast cancer survivor. It was also a celebration for the birthday I share with Claudette.

Claudette and her daughter, Cimone, were my surprise gifts. I was extremely happy to see both of them. I missed them. We enjoyed our dinner talking and laughing as we shared what we'd learned from my breast cancer journey. Claudette did not speak, but her eyes and uncomfortable demeanor told me what I already knew. It's all good.

My love for butterflies was the theme that night. My friends shared poetry associated with the life of a butterfly and how my growth throughout this experience paralleled it. Some of my gifts even reflected the butterfly theme, such as the five-hundred-piece butterfly puzzle from my friend Te-mika.

Later, my friends really enjoyed the challenge of putting it together. The big snowstorm in February 2010 provided the opportunity. Everyone was snowed in because the whole region was buried under more than three feet of snow. Still, my friends and neighbors managed to dig their way out to visit. For hours, at least four to five people worked together on that butterfly puzzle. What a fun time we had. Te-mika's wonderful gift made us all happy during then. Not to mention the (group) therapy it provided. No amount of psychological therapy sessions could provide the same results as that snowstorm/puzzle assembly party. It was a beautiful time.

I always viewed my co-worker and friend Lane as a person who fully embraced life. One day, I received a package that she and my friend Margo sent. In it I found a coloring book, colored pencils, and *Origami Classroom II* by Dokuotei Nakano. This was a kit with a how-to book and sixty sheets of specially designed, rainbow-colored paper for creating origami accent models such as flowers, finger puppets, airplanes, flapping birds, and more. The kit was exactly the therapy I needed. My friends also enjoyed the challenge of creating some of the models. This was by far the most relaxing activity in my recovery process.

My colleagues in human resources and other coworkers understood how challenging it was for me to manage the work/life balance while dealing with a significant illness. I remember one very special occasion that my dear friend and co-worker, Gloria, had initiated in honor of me. Gloria and I always worked well together, and we shared our personal lives as well. Gloria understood clearly what I was going through because she had family members who had experienced breast cancer. She was very supportive throughout my entire process and always seemed to sense when I wasn't feeling well, no matter how hard I tried to be strong. Gloria's constant insistence that I take care of myself first was right on point because I had far more healing to do than I ever could have imagined.

At that time, human resources had a lot of initiatives going on and most of us barely had time to take a lunch break. Nevertheless, Gloria e-mailed staff members to see who might be available for some fruit and other goodies in celebration of our hard work. I thought this was a great idea and long overdue. Little did I know this special occasion was actually planned for me. I arrived late to the conference room, but just in time for everyone to let me know that the get-together honoring us was actually a ploy for everyone to get together to honor me.

The surprise was such a humbling experience. Everyone told me that I was an inspiration to them and that they admired my positive attitude and strength while going through this difficult time in my life. That was such an emotional moment for most of us in the conference room. I was presented with a spa gift certificate and cards. To this day, I can't believe I missed knowing what was going on behind my back.

This act of kindness came at a time when I needed it most. Up until this point, I had forgotten to cry. I had maintained a constant state of motion to get through it, and I did not allow myself any release until this point. I really needed this celebration for cleansing my mind, body, and soul.

Support continued to make a difference in my wellness process when five of my girlfriends waited for me after the lumpectomy surgery. What a surprise to see them when I came home! Some of my girlfriends were in my kitchen cooking, while others were the sunroom. After a short visit with them, my husband escorted me upstairs to our bedroom so I could rest. He propped up the pillows behind me and put a light blanket over me. Byrd went to work shortly after, and my girlfriends continued their visit.

In fact, they blew up an air mattress and placed it on my bedroom floor because they spent the night while Byrd was working the overnight shift. One girlfriend slept in my black rocking chair, the one that Byrd and I purchased when we first started dating. (This was also the chair we rocked both our boys in when they were babies.) Another girlfriend curled up in our chocolate-colored chaise lounge. The whole scene was so comforting. We talked and laughed throughout the night. I eventually drifted off into a peaceful sleep. Life couldn't have been any better than at that moment. True friendships are priceless, particularly at a time like this.

I know I am blessed to receive so much love and support—a healing medicine that gave me hope and strength. I learned, whether you have support or not, you must believe in yourself. Have faith that your positive outlook will get you through your breast cancer journey. You are not alone if you trust and feel safe with your professional medical staff, helpful support groups, and other breast cancer patients or survivors!

I believe support is critical to healing and advancing to the next step in your life. I also believe that helping others through outreach and being transparent with your personal experience has its own special healing powers. Making the best of this opportunity to learn, grow, and embrace your wellness journey can help you toward a better recovery.

Chapter Five

Healing with Humor and Humility

A sense of humor and humility in the face of life's unexpected situations is essential. Life was not dark and gloomy as I progressed through my wellness journey. In fact, one of my remedies for healing was lots of humor. My day was not complete without a hearty laugh. It didn't matter if it was about something simple or just about me. Humor and laughter gave me such uplift and hope that tomorrow would be better than yesterday.

With or Without Gravy

Claudette (aka "Dette") is funny without even realizing it. She can be direct, but she has a kind heart and giving spirit. And she is definitely Miss Drama Queen. She would have a different opinion, of course, and tell me, "You've got your nerve, Sister!" While we share similar wonderful qualities, we are quite different.

When Claudette was available, she would come over to visit and assist me with whatever I needed. She would answer my door when people came to visit or to drop off a meal. On one particular day, I was upstairs in bed when I heard Claudette open the door and greet one of my girlfriends. Claudette kindly invited her in, and they exchanged pleasantries.

My visitor told Claudette she had prepared meat loaf, vegetables, and mashed potatoes, and she hoped I would be able to eat it. I heard Claudette say in a playful manner, "Girl, is this meatloaf with or without gravy? God knows I can't fix any gravy! I usually buy gravy in a jar because who's gonna know?" At that moment I heard a rumbling noise like someone was fumbling through a bag. From out of that bag, my girlfriend pulled the same brand of gravy that Claudette buys. The two of them were hilariously tickled and they began giving each other high fives and laughing so loud that they didn't even notice I was part of the laughter, too. They laughed about their gravy secret, as if they were the only two who knew. They decided that their mothers, who had taught them how to make gravy from scratch, would still approve of them for finding a shortcut. Claudette made my day and didn't even know it. I am thankful for the great laugh therapy.

Minus One Red Sandal

"Miss! Oh, miss! Miss, did you lose a red flip-flop sandal?"

I immediately thought, *What in the world is she talking about?* But I looked down at my feet, and I was wearing only one red sandal. I couldn't believe it! I was so embarrassed. The woman said she found my sandal in aisle six, where I had been a few moments before. It dawned on me why a couple of other customers had looked at me strangely. Lord, have mercy!

This incident happened during chemotherapy, when I had a severe case of peripheral neuropathy. The numbness occurred during my visit to the supermarket and impaired my brain's ability to recognize that there was no shoe on my cold foot. Wow! I couldn't believe neither my girlfriend nor I noticed.

Well, what's a girl to do? I put the shoe back on, and my girlfriend and I laughed all the way to the checkout counter. I learned firsthand that humor is a necessary accessory for all difficult journeys and laughter has healing powers. Like any well-dressed woman, I was properly accessorized for my journey.

Hair Attack

Now here is a "hot mess" situation. Lorrie and Bennie are friends of ours who decided to get married. By the date of their wedding, I could not comb or brush my hair because it was all falling out. As their wedding planner, I prayed that this would not happen. I didn't wear a wig, so I banked on wearing the beautiful, elegant hat my dear friends Pat and Larry purchased for me at the Proper Topper store in Washington, DC. They wanted to make sure I protected myself from the sun as much as possible because they knew the wedding was outdoors. Unfortunately, it was very windy the day of the wedding, so I was unable to wear the hat. I put the hat in my car for safekeeping.

Plan A, which was the hat, didn't work. So I had to come up with a plan B. With limited time to think, this was definitely a challenge. I had to get creative in a hurry. I had a clipboard in my right hand and, while lining up the bridal party, I thought, *Yes, just causally place your left hand over the bald spot, and no one will notice.*

This was a nightmare. I heard my husband, my twin, and my girlfriend all say, "Go sit down; we've got this for you." *Oh no, I don't think so—not after my nine months of planning this event.* Planning Lorrie and Bennie's wedding truly was great therapy during my chemotherapy process. It kept me focused on the couple and not on my pain. My goal was to successfully execute Lori and Bennie's wedding as planned.

As I was ready to send the first bridesmaid down the outdoor aisle, the person playing the music signaled to me. He was confused about which track to play for the bridal party. Immediately, I hurried over to the other side of the pavilion and totally forgot about my plan B. The music was squared away, and I proceeded to signal the bridesmaids to begin their walk.

But wait—I felt something fuzzy in the top of my sundress. And no, it was not chest hair. Now, to know me is to know that, at this particular moment, I would usually have run past the crowd, screaming and trying to shake out whatever was in my dress. But this would most certainly have taken away from the elegance of the celebration. I remained cool. I indiscreetly shook my dress, oh so slightly twisting and wiggling. Finally, I could see that it was my loose hair that had fallen into my sundress. I noticed a couple of people looking at me and smiling. I wonder if they thought I was grooving to the music.

After the wedding ceremony was over, when everyone was enjoying the reception dinner, I went to the car mirror to check out the bald spot. Oh, good gracious! There was nothing I could even conceive of to cover that big ol' bald patch. Instead, I had a nice glass of wine and enjoyed the lovely atmosphere.

Oops, I Broke My Ankle

Being from Kansas, I love snow. In February of 2010, when some two feet of snow fell in a matter of hours, I wanted to play in the snow because I felt I was continuing to heal from chemotherapy and radiation and getting stronger by the day. It has always been a tradition in my community, especially on my block, that all of the neighbors get together after a snowstorm to help shovel all the neighbors' driveways, clear the sidewalks, and dig out the cars.

Byrd was being very protective of me and, especially during my treatments, asked me to remain inside the house to avoid falling on the ice. Well, there was one particular day when I had cabin fever so bad that I wrapped myself up, put on my boots, and went out the door to partake in some fresh air. It felt like I had been inside for months, leaving only to go to my doctor's appointments.

All the neighbors looked forward to pitching in to help each other remove the snow. And we used the time to have fun in all that fresh, fluffy, white stuff. Children frolicked, and teens engaged in animated snowball fights. We took pictures throughout the day of our snowy, fun activities. Over the years, all the neighbors and the Cheverly community in general, have developed a special bond, enjoying the family focused benefits offered by this charming, friendly town.

Taking in the clean, fresh air was awesome, and I wanted more. So the next night, around midnight, several friends wanted to have a snowball battle. We stood outside, planning our teams and our strategies. I took one step forward, heard a loud *crack* sound, and down to the ground I went. It happened so fast. I knew my ankle was either sprained or broken. Everyone rushed to help me back to my house. I didn't recognize the pain from the fall because every day, from sun up to sun down, I had pain throughout most of my body. Two days later, I went to the emergency room at Doctors Community Hospital. The verdict: broken ankle.

I was sent home with a splint and instructions to see a foot and ankle specialist at MedStar Georgetown University Hospital. The color of my cast was baby blue. I never adjusted to using crutches or a walker because those were too awkward to manage. Besides, one day while using the walker, it jammed in my bathroom doorframe. I couldn't move it or myself until one of my sons finally came to my rescue. I must have been stuck in that doorway for fifteen minutes, calling out for help. Okay, maybe it was more like two minutes. My dear sons, ears plugged, were listening to music and didn't hear my cries for help. That whole episode was a mess! Needless to say, the walker did not last long at all.

This Was No Accident

Months after I was diagnosed with breast cancer, my job was eliminated, along with many others. This was another unexpected, major life change that I was challenged with. I was shocked! I hadn't seen this coming. Well, of course I hadn't; I had been on medical leave. Minutes after receiving this news from my employer, I knew God had another plan for me. Even though I enjoyed my job, I also embraced the opportunity for new adventures. I now had the freedom to heal without worry or stress. God had changed my direction to accommodate his plans and not mine. Blessings come in many ways. *This was no accident.*

It was either the first or second week in December of 2008 when my employer notified me that my job was eliminated. I had just finished the chemotherapy treatments at the end of November 2008, was still suffering from side effects, and was being prepped for radiation treatments. I was eager to get home from the grocery store because I felt physically and emotionally exhausted, and the ever-present pain was settling in my bones that cold afternoon.

There was a woman I did not recognize in the parking lot that day. She began waving at me with enthusiasm. I wondered, *Why is this strange woman waving at me? I don't know her. I have already waved back to her twice while backing out of the parking space. I'll just ignore her, and I'm sure she'll go away.* I continued backing out. *Oh my, I hope she isn't crazy.* If I were still living in Topeka, where people are just that friendly, I wouldn't question her waving at me. But in the city, I have become a little more cautious.

I continued backing out of my parking space, and the woman waved a third time. She was trying desperately to get my attention. By the time I realized why she was trying to get my attention, it was too late. I backed my car into the passenger side of a young woman's car. This was the first time I had ever hit someone's car, and thank God, no one was hurt. We both exited our cars to assess the damage and exchange information. The other driver was quite upset, and as we talked her volume continued to elevate. She kept saying, "I don't need this. I don't need this!"

At that moment, my pain and aggravation overpowered me, and I shouted back, "And I don't need this cancer!" I realized that I was angry about having cancer and tired of the pain. I had never reacted this way until then. I thought I had it under control and understood that blessings can be found in both pain and joy. This incident was no accident.

"I'm sorry, I didn't mean to complain. It's just that I thought doctors were supposed to make you feel better and not worse," she said. She was suffering from Crohn's disease and, after having an episode, she had been released from the hospital that morning. She shared with me how she could barely make it to the store because of her pain level. Her father had been released from the hospital the night before after suffering a sudden heart attack, and her mother had been admitted to the hospital one day prior after suffering a stroke. I was devastated for her. My heart sank.

Standing against the driver's side of her car, she slid down to the ground, crying uncontrollably. It wasn't about the accident anymore; it was about embracing someone whose pain and suffering seemed far greater than my own. *Dear God, what is this journey about?* The police arrived at the accident scene, and the officer questioned why he had been called, based on our interaction with each other. Everything was settled, and before we parted, we hugged tightly. We exchanged telephone numbers, and I invited her to my church. This was no accident.

What a crazy time. I was processing all that had happened within those last two weeks, and then the accident happened. I asked, *God, is there any way you can go easy on me this week?* I forgot to cry.

Healing comes in many forms. I have always appreciated that humor is downright good therapy. Its physical and emotional healing powers can lead to unknowable wellness. In my situation, I lived daily to laugh at myself, even when I was at my worst. My friends told me all the time, "You make us forget that you are ill because you constantly keep us laughing."

Laughter needs no prescription. It's a free dose of feeling good. It's yours to embrace whenever you need encouragement.

CHAPTER SIX

Who Needs Hair?

My hair has always been my crown jewel. All my life, I've been fortunate to have healthy, thick hair. I took full advantage of my hair, wearing it in the various current styles over the years or creating my own look. I used potions and lotions to tame my hair and hats and wraps to add flair. I loved my hair, and my hair loved me. Knowing that losing my hair was a likely side effect of the treatments, I had resolved that I would have to say good-bye to my hair, at least for a while. I thought maybe I should go wig shopping.

Monica and I worked together. When she joined the human resources department, we connected immediately, and we have been close friends ever since. She introduced me to her family at the wig shop in Annapolis, Maryland.

"Monica, what do you think about this wig?" I asked her while browsing in the wig shop in Annapolis. "Is it the right style and color for my complexion?" I asked. She said it looked good, but she also encouraged her husband to share his opinion. Monica's husband, Lake, and their eleven-month-old daughter, Nile, hung out with us that day. I don't know how many wigs we both tried on, but we had a blast. Even Nile looked darling in some of the styles. We laughed as we watched her having a good time.

The owner of the shop, to whom MedStar Georgetown University Hospital refers cancer patients, commented on how positive I was during this phase of my treatment process. At that time, several other women were in the shop looking for a wig to match their hair before it started coming out. They were frustrated and appeared sad because of the circumstances. Perhaps if they were more accepting and embracing of this change, the shopping might have gone more smoothly. I did purchase a wig that day, but I only wore it to the International World Bank Christmas party that winter. I must admit, it was fun to wear that one time. It also kept my head warm on that icy cold night.

Pat knew I was planning and coordinating the wedding for Lorrie and Bennie. She was concerned about my energy level and how I was going to protect myself from the sun on the afternoon of the wedding. If she weren't going to be out of town that weekend, Pat would have been happy to assist me with the wedding. In the past, Pat and I have teamed up to work on many projects, including planning special events. She was more than capable of helping me and producing excellent results. Byrd, Claudette, and my girlfriend Carolyn provided excellent assistance for Lorrie and Bennie's wedding that day.

Pat called me about two weeks before the wedding to inquire about my choice of headdress to shield me from the sun on the day of the wedding. "None," I replied. I actually had not thought that much about my wardrobe for the day. Pat and Larry asked me to visit the Proper Topper online store and choose a hat. I selected a beautiful topper that would serve the double duty of being stylish and providing much needed coverage for my head. I thank Pat and Larry for making me feel so special. They both are such generous people. As I mentioned earlier, it ended up being extremely windy the day of the wedding, so I was unable to wear my lovely hat on that day. But I still love that hat, and since then, I have worn that hat with special pride.

The day after Lorrie and Bennie's wedding, my hair fell out almost completely. When I woke up, I saw my hair all over the bed. I kept massaging my head, taking in the baldness. Then I collected it, made a ball out of it, and tossed it on my husband. Byrd didn't even have to ask me if I was ready to go to the barber shop, he already knew the answer. He said that going to the barber shop was one of the happier times for him because it was another opportunity for us to share this process together. Chris, our barber, was proud that I chose him to shave my head bald. Byrd videotaped my experience. It is all good! After all, who needs hair?

Shaving my head meant that I was confident, strong, and ready to be transparent. I totally embraced the new me; I felt liberated. After Chris finished shaving my head, I experienced the core essence of me. What a good feeling.

Our good friends, Sonjai and Lloyd, who live in our neighborhood, were the first to see me with a bald head. When Sonjai and I first met, we felt like kindred sisters. Byrd and Lloyd became good friends as well. We knocked on their door that Sunday morning, and they both came to the door screaming with pride and joy that I took such a bold step. They both said the look suited me well. They took pictures of me and my husband.

I was glad they were the first to see me because we have a deep and comfortable relationship in which we embrace each other's spirits with lots of love. I thank them for all the wonderful dinners and relaxing times we shared. They are both very special folks. I will always cherish our friendship with much love.

The next day, I went to work, and many people applauded me for being brave enough to go completely bald. They said I inspired them because I embraced the changes I was going through, plus I wore baldness well. Going bald completely exposed me. I was so happy with this change. For the first time in my life, I was 100 percent ready to accept me without any hang-ups! What an uplift this was in my process. Each day, my bald head was a new experience for me. I had my head shaved three times before I began to let it grow out for the winter.

Monee, whom I affectionately call "MoMo," has more hair than the law allows. She has huge hair! At times, it can overpower her petite frame, particularly when she does not relax her natural curls. When she wears her hair naturally curly, it's like a flashback to a 1960s afro on steroids. Um, can you say "Woodstock"?

Monee is a free spirit and loves having fun. She and I have been neighbors and friends for about four years as of the writing of this book. We both attended Zion Church, where we were members of the small life group, which was lead by Monee. She is also a growing Christian and disciple.

I asked her to quote a scripture from the Bible regarding the value of hair. She suggested the following: "Do not let your adornment be merely outward—arranging the hair, wearing the gold, or putting on fine apparel—rather let it be the hidden person of the heart, with the incorruptible beauty of a gentle and quiet spirit, which is very precious in the sight of God."

(1 Peter 3:3). This scripture truly validates my point. Who needs hair? It is inner beauty that defines our character.

To this day, I admire anyone who is brave enough to shave his or her head, regardless of the reason. I believe change is necessary to grow. Be not afraid of who you are or the possibility of creating a new you. Besides, who needs hair? I thank God that I didn't rely on my hair to define who I am.

CHAPTER SEVEN

Healing with Passion and Purpose

When my job was eliminated in January 2009, I was slowly healing from the chemotherapy and being prepped for the radiation treatments. During my healing process at home, I determined that creating outreach efforts and participating in the breast cancer community was now my calling.

My first priority was to serve as a breast cancer advocate. Sharing my testimony as a breast cancer survivor, I became a guest speaker and served as a panelist for local hospitals, churches, small groups, and other venues. Being transparent about my wellness journey was healing for me. Also, despite my pain and suffering, it became beneficial for me to inspire, give hope, and encourage women who were going through a similar breast cancer journey.

I was trained at MedStar Georgetown University Hospital to become a mentor for newly diagnosed patients. I joined Georgetown University's Lombardi Comprehensive Cancer Center's Sisters Informing Sisters group and participated in the Stepping Stone pilot study for cancer survivors on maintaining their wellness through nutrition and exercise. In the near future, this study will provide opportunities for mentoring and coaching other women selected to participate in this study. I also participate in clinical studies in an effort to make a difference in the cancer world.

My family and friends refer people they know who have been diagnosed with cancer, or who have survived it, to me so I can provide them with support and inspiration. I maintain a list of these women who hail from different parts of the United States, and I talk with them from time to time.

For as long as I can remember, one of my passions has been interior design. I have wanted to find a way to incorporate my design talent with a cancer outreach resource. It is important for me to use my God-given talent to serve the cancer community.

I recall clearly when Byrd and I began discussing the addition of a sunroom. He asked me what the main purpose of the room would be. I believed that the room would be a comfortable retreat space where family and friends could relax and enjoy themselves for hours. I designed this room with lots of plants, candles, and accessories. We frequently had music flowing throughout the room to recognize my husband's appreciation for the arts.

The more I relaxed and healed in our sunroom, the more I listened to God. I knew that my life had changed and that I was now a living testimony. It was clear that I needed to give back in some way and that my passion could support and foster hope for women going through their wellness journeys.

One day, while walking around my house, I realized that each room really made me feel uplifted in some way. Each room gave a feeling of warmth and comfort. For more than twenty years, I've loved interior design. During those years, I've transformed the spaces in the homes of family and friends by using their existing furniture, relocating accessories, adding color, repurposing curtains, and adding or moving art. I believe that a changed space helps create a changed attitude for moving forward in life.

While observing that family and friends who visited me in my sunroom stayed positive about my situation, a light bulb went on, so to speak. Why not start an interior design company with a focus on repurposing and home staging? Yes, this felt right, and I decided to take an international professional repurposing/home staging interior design course to add credibility to my twenty years of practical experience.

After completing my course work, I officially created my company, Endless Expressions Interior Design, where our motto is "Healing Starts at Home." Endless Expressions Interior Design services are offered to anyone seeking change and renewal. The goal of a changed environment is to create a renewed energy for your life by incorporating your unique style in your space.

When asked to be a guest speaker for a breast cancer focus group, I offer a special drawing for a free healing-room makeover. My husband and I furnish the paint for the room if the winner chooses to have the room painted. Most patients do because color has a strong psychological impact for change and healing.

Spending time with other breast cancer patients and survivors and listening to their journey while sharing mine, is healing. It is not unusual for me to receive feedback such as, "I would never have thought this piece of furniture would work in this space," and "I never imaged this color would make this room so special and make me feel so blessed." It is my passion and purpose to share my gifts to help someone renew his or her space or create a healing environment while he or she is going through a wellness process.

Making a difference with patients and survivors through re-purposing their spaces is an important step in helping them to embrace their journeys. Talk about creative therapy! Again, to see and hear how patient's re-purposed space has inspired his or her changed attitude for a hopeful tomorrow is extremely gratifying. I know I have, in some way, made a difference.

My passion and skill for interior design also led me to create workshops for cancer patients and survivors. These workshops teach how to design a healing room while going through wellness.

I continue to seek opportunities to inspire and encourage people going through the breast cancer journey. Another reason I chose to write *I Forgot to Cry* was to share my experience in the hope of making someone's journey a little brighter.

CHAPTER EIGHT

On the Road to Healing

Talk about good therapy! Finally being able to travel and see my family and friends gave me the boost I needed for healing.

In May 2009, I was excited to travel to Chicago for the sixtieth birthday celebration of my older twin sisters, Paula and Wanda. Though I was still weak and tired, my source of strength was connecting with family. Their love and inspiration has always given me hope. Oh, how I so looked forward to being with family! We laugh uncontrollably, talk into the night, eat good food, and shower each other with love. I knew, regardless of how I was feeling, that my healing would continue because I would be surrounded by family. Paula and Wanda's birthday celebration was a bash, and I could not imagine not being there to support them. Family is my heart.

In retrospect, I am happy that I did not share everything about my condition with my family while going through my chemotherapy and radiation treatment process. There were many times the pain and suffering were so unbearable that I could hardly sleep, eat, or walk.

I did not want to add any more stress to my family and friends because I knew God was my deliverance from what He designed for me in the first place. My siblings would have preferred that I shared everything with them. However, there was no way I could continue to interrupt their lives and have them focus on me 24/7 with so much worry and concern. Byrd and I agreed that, if there were a significant change in my health, we would share it with my siblings.

About a month after returning from the birthday celebration, my girlfriend Carolyn and I drove to Greensboro, North Carolina, to visit our girlfriend Doretta. It had been at least five years since we'd seen Doretta. In that time, Doretta's husband died, her mother had a major stroke that paralyzed her from the waist down, and Doretta was managing some other critical family matters. Doretta was the primary caretaker for her mother. She no longer had the flexibility to travel, so Carolyn and I drove to visit. I was getting stronger and felt excited to see her.

Doretta, whom I affectionately call "Dee," became one of my closest and dearest friends. I met her through Byrd; as children, their families lived across the street from one another. Both were only children in their families, so they bonded like sister and brother. When I met Doretta while dating my husband, she and I connected instantly and become close friends. She moved to Greensboro many years ago, but we've always kept in touch.

When Doretta learned of my diagnosis, she couldn't believe it. "My nerves were out of control," she said, "but I pulled myself together because I knew that Nia was a fighter, and we were going to see this through. She was not going anywhere."

Doretta struggled with living so far away and not being available for me. When we spoke on the telephone, she could sense the pain in my voice even though I remained upbeat. While she knew I had a host of people supporting me, she felt she wasn't giving her all because she was away from the area. All she wanted was to hold and comfort me when I needed strength. Doretta openly shared her concerns about my surgeries and treatments. Truth has always been the foundation of our relationship. We understand and expect each other to be straightforward. Doretta knows that I am a fighter and that I would tell her if things were not going well.

Doretta recommended several cancer organizations and other resources that I could contact regarding my wellness. I thank Doretta for always being resourceful. My illness hit very close to home for her. She never thought about it much before, but she came to realize the importance of immediately contacting a doctor when you feel something is amiss with your body. Life is short, and you have to live every moment to the fullest. "Tomorrow is not a promise, so you have to enjoy your time and the people around you. Girl, you are a testimony in and of yourself," she said. "Only you and I understand that statement." That's right. Like sisters away from home, we can always count on each other.

Our visit with Doretta was very healing, peaceful, and fun. We stayed with her for five days and had a great time. Carolyn and I tried to help Doretta de-clutter her home and repurpose some of her rooms. Ah, what great therapy this was for me because I love interior design and helping someone else feel good. Our efforts went well for a few days before Doretta began to resist: She wasn't ready to interrupt the surroundings that brought her comfort. Doretta just wanted to enjoy our company.

Greensboro is beautiful. Driving along the countryside was inspirational; it reminded me to take time to smell the roses and enjoy nature. This trip was so relaxing that I could have stayed for another week. The road trip was proof that, despite any challenges, keeping the faith and embracing those wonderful moments is what a purposeful journey is about.

I couldn't believe my class reunion in Topeka was just a few months after visiting Doretta. I continued to feel stronger over time, so my twin Claudette and I decided to attend our class reunion in August. This trip was especially important because it meant going back to my hometown and to my family and friends. Trust me, I will always cherish my roots and the love of my extended family and friends.

Members of my hometown church, Saint John AME, sent cards and called to give me words of encouragement during my treatments. My brother, Dale, and sister-in-law, Anita, updated the church members on my condition. The church kept me in prayer. I will always be grateful to Saint John's for embracing me and my family as we grew up in the church and continued to serve the Lord.

What a wonderful feeling to be around friends I've known since first grade at Highland Park School. In school, Claudette and I had been popular because we were kind-hearted, loving, and fun. We were raised to value and respect people of different cultures. That is why going to a predominately white school was of no concern to us. Our experience with diversity was all good.

I learned at our class reunion mixer that several classmates had been stricken with cancer. Interestingly, they were all men. They openly shared their journeys battling different types of cancer. That was surprising. Men don't always talk about their health challenges, and certainly not their emotions while going through the experiences. I was truly inspired by their testimonies. They looked healthy and well.

Visiting my hometown was special. My pain and suffering seemed to take a backseat to the joy of spending time with family and old friends. My time was limited, and I truly wanted to make the most of my visit. I scheduled a spa visit for my twin and me before we left to return home. The unexpected blessing was the masseuse, Valeria, who was a cancer survivor as well. Valeria knew exactly how to bring relief to the pain in my extremities caused by the peripheral neuropathy. The nerve damage in my hands and feet from the chemotherapy drugs did a number on me. The massage session was such a treat, not to mention wonderful physical and mental therapy. In fact, my one-hour massage ran over an additional fifteen minutes. Valeria and I are both believers in faith, so we instantly bonded. We even talked about collaborating on some outreach opportunities in Topeka. God makes no mistake about the people He brings to your life.

My final two trips of 2009 were spent at the beach in North Carolina's Outer Banks. The first trip in September was when I began to record my breast cancer journey, and the second trip was during the Thanksgiving holiday week. My travels that summer of 2009 proved to be so healing. They gave me the hope and faith I needed to continue believing that everything would be all right.

CHAPTER NINE

Faith over Fear

Before breast cancer, I never considered that my life would change without me controlling that change. It never occurred to me that I would become the woman I have seen so many times with her head shaved or with no facial hair at all. *Who am I?* was the question I asked constantly throughout my process. I looked to find me, but I slowly leaned toward the idea of creating a new me. My journey was out of my control, and during the early part of my treatment process, I did not like that feeling of vulnerability.

After everything, I was exhausted. I believed that if I kept moving, I wouldn't have to deal with all the aches and pains. The pain and suffering were overwhelming. But I didn't cry. After I finished the chemotherapy and radiation treatments, I realized crying was an essential part of therapy; it represented cleansing and renewing of the mind, body, and spirit. Before this time, I focused on being positive and avoided crying as a way to prevent further stress and sadness for myself, family, and friends. I felt I needed to remain strong for all of us in order to get through this process successfully. Or was it that I really was far too exhausted to release the emotion?

In my moments of doubt, there was a scripture in the *New Spirit-Filled Life Bible (NKJV)*, the New King James Version, that I referred to when I needed to restore my faith.

> And He said unto me, "My grace is sufficient for you, for My
> strength is made perfect in weakness." Therefore, most gladly

"I will rather boast in my infirmities, that the power of Christ may rest upon me." (2 Corinthians12:9)

I know that the trials and tribulations I have gone through are temporary and purposeful. In my process, I have learned to live by faith because God's grace is sufficient in all situations. My spiritual growth has far exceeded anything I experienced before my breast cancer journey. Since then, I have become a small group leader for my church at Zion. I never thought of serving in that capacity because I felt I needed to know scripture. I was wrong; this position called for meeting God, growing closer to God, and serving God. If I didn't have this experience, my trust and faith in God would not have been at the level it is now. Guess what? God knew exactly what He had in store for me long before I did.

After my unexpected experience with breast cancer, I had to find myself and weigh how I could move forward. I struggled to find my "normal," but it wasn't quite there. All the things in life that were comfortable to me remained the same, yet my whole perspective was much more tentative.

As a cancer survivor, my life now has more meaning than I could have ever imagined. I thought my pre-cancer life was wonderful, filled as it was with the love of family and friends. Apparently, God had something more, something different, for me.

The reality of being a breast cancer patient and survivor was overwhelming at times. A year had passed since my surgeries, physical therapy, chemotherapy, and radiation. I was on the road to healing, but I wasn't moving nearly as fast as I wanted. I wanted so desperately to regain full control of my life and not to have the illness dictate my path.

My journey has taught me to believe strongly in faith over fear because faith has healing powers. I learned that it takes patience for healing both physically and mentally. It was critical for advancing to the next level in my life.

There were times during my healing process that I had some serious reality checks. I allowed my fear to overwhelm me at times. If I had placed my faith and trust in God, I would have acknowledged who was in charge, and it wasn't me. My inspiration for healing came from so many sources, including God. I was inspired by reading my Bible as well as the beautiful, inspirational cards sent by family, friends, and co-workers. These readings only confirmed to me that everything would be as God intended. What a blessing! I know the will of God will never take me where the grace of God will not protect me.

I truly have a deeper appreciation for life. It's funny, the little things that used to bother me are no longer so important. But, the things I placed on hold, saying that I would get to them one day, have become more important to accomplish.

My journey taught me to live well, to laugh (uncontrollably at all times), and to celebrate life every chance I have an opportunity. It taught me that obstacles are only opportunities for growth and that I should never settle for anything that I do not feel passionate about. By the end of my treatment process, I stopped trying to find myself. Instead, I am excited about who I have become.

I believe my setback was designed by God to be a comeback for new beginnings. The truth is that some of the things we learn come through pain and suffering. The benefits can prepare us to serve others in a way that will provide hope for a brighter tomorrow.

Writing this book has been an inspirational and healing process. There is no way I could keep this experience to myself. My hope for sharing my journey is that I can encourage cancer patients, survivors, family members, and friends to know that they are not alone when facing a similar journey.

My journey has taught me that there is advantage in our weakness and that there is blessing in our pain; when I felt helpless, my faith caused me to lean on God's grace to sustain me.

Whatever circumstances you are facing, I believe that cleansing your mind, body, and spirit moves you forward to advancing to the next step in life. Everyone needs some measure of healing. Throughout my journey, discovering ways of healing helped me to believe there is a better tomorrow. I realized that only going through the motions within my process blocked my emotions. *I forgot to cry.* Concealing emotions can make the healing recovery a little longer. I learned that releasing my tears during a challenging situation can be cleansing to the mind, body, and spirit. I understand this now.

****

Thank you, God, for blessing me with the words to write my first book!

TRIBUTE TO FAMILY
AND FRIENDS

Thank you, dear family and friends, for being a part of my breast cancer journey because you were in it for the long run. Words cannot express how grateful and blessed my family and I are to have had you in our lives throughout the years. Your acts of kindness, thoughtfulness, and support gave me the strength I needed to complete a successful treatment process. You were my healing medicine, and my journey would not have been complete without you.

There was no way I wasn't going to acknowledge your faithful commitment; your love and support embraced me with special healing blessings. Part of being strong throughout my process is attributable to the power of your love and support. It gave me encouragement to never give up. You inspired me to continue my journey for a brighter tomorrow.

Love, Nia

ADDENDUM
INTERVIEW QUESTIONS

A couple of years after my surgeries and treatment process, I asked my family and friends how they faced my illness and the impact it had on their life. This was probably one of the toughest parts of writing this book. Asking each of them to revisit a time of uncertainty during my journey was heartbreaking. We all needed some measure of healing in order to find closure.

Therefore, the timing of when to capture their interviews was very important. Initially, when I asked for everyone's responses to my interview questions, I couldn't deliver these questions without revealing my pain. But months later, after continuing to heal with time, I was ready to ask my questions without feeling sad.

Siblings

Claudette and I were born five minutes apart. Our personalities are just as different as they are similar. I asked Claudette about her initial reaction upon learning of my diagnosis. She said, "I was shocked and saddened." Claudette did not come to the biopsy procedure because she had previously scheduled appointments. My older sisters, Paula and Wanda, told Claudette the outcome of the biopsy. I know the revelation of her twin being diagnosed with cancer was quite frightening for her. Even though she was in disbelief, Claudette said, "I believed that God had already healed you and the rest was just a minor detour."

Claudette said, "Being your twin, I felt your pain, discomfort, and worry throughout your process. It was an out-of-body experience that I really cannot put into words—a unique trait shared amongst twins." I felt Claudette's pain for me, and I knew it was very difficult at times for her to spend time with me.

Claudette also had some physical challenges going on at that time. I felt bad because I was unable to reach out to her as I normally would have. Truthfully, I could barely wrap my head around the unknown outcome I was facing. I could only imagine what Claudette's thoughts might have been regarding the possibility of life without her twin. A thousand what-ifs must have run through her mind. I never asked Claudette about it because I knew it would bring back the raw emotions from that time. For the most part, Claudette kept her emotions under control, but at times, they would slip out.

For Claudette, as it was for others, my battle with breast cancer truly helped her put things into perspective and really understands how fragile life can be. Her new goal became to live life as if every day were her last and continuing to do whatever made her happy. That's my twin!

Cimone, Claudette's daughter, was also surprised when she learned I was diagnosed with breast cancer. She didn't really know what to think. All she could do at that point was pray to God and ask that He see me through. When asked what reactions she observed of her mother while I was going through my wellness journey, Cimone said, "Like any sibling, she was very concerned about your well-being. The only difference is you two are twins, so the feelings are perhaps even stronger."

Cimone noticed that her mom would sometimes feel what I was feeling and even had some of the side effects that a patient might experience from chemotherapy. I wasn't aware that this was happening to Claudette. "I knew that my mom had your best interests at heart and that she wanted nothing more than for you to be delivered from having breast cancer." Being a twin is a special blessing, especially when your twin takes on your emotions and chemotherapy's side effects. That is something amazing. Claudette truly kept her end of the bargain as my other half. Cimone knew that everything was in God's hands. My situation impacted Cimone's life by reinforcing how important family is and that, when a crisis happens, family will be there for support like no one else can be.

Paula and Wanda were born sixteen months before Claudette and me. We sisters affectionately call Paula by the name "McBee." She lives in

Tempe, Arizona. God picked a good one when He added Paula to the family. She is an attractive woman with a kind spirit. She has a low-key demeanor and is quite a patient person.

Paula admitted that she was devastated to hear that her baby sister's tumor was cancerous. After her initial shock, Paula recalled what our father went through during his battle with pancreatic cancer. She knew, because I am our father's daughter, that I, too, would be strong. Paula and I talked on the phone for many hours about my experience throughout my wellness journey, and we caught up on what was happening in her life as well. I am truly blessed to have my sisters as my best friends.

Paula always sent me beautiful inspirational cards; she even sent a warm, fuzzy bed jacket along with other items to keep my spirits lifted. I remember one card in particular that specifically addressed my cancer. Paula was not afraid to say the "C" word around me. She later shared with me that Fred, her husband, had a fit because he felt Paula was not being sensitive.

Paula said that my breast cancer journey has made her more aware of what is going on with her own body. Her doctor in Arizona continues to monitor her health closely given the fact that I had breast cancer. I send Paula much love always. Through thick and thin, we are family.

Fred also provided strong support for my family. Fred is a well-rounded person who appreciates life. He is a humble man and is always there when you need him. I was glad both Paula and Fred came for my biopsy procedure because they wanted to hear firsthand exactly what was going on and what the next steps were in my treatment process. Fred was a special blessing to Byrd, who was doing his best to comprehend my situation.

Fred was also a special blessing to me. When Paula wasn't home to receive my calls, Fred would sense I needed to talk, and he was there for me. We would talk about everything, including pain, glory, and what a blessing life is. Because of Fred's own health issues, he fully understood what managing a chronic illness is about. Fred is my favorite brother-in-law; could it be because he is the only one standing? (Family joke!)

Paula and Wanda were born twenty minutes apart. Wanda is affectionately known to me as "Wanna." Wanda is unlike her twin, who is cool and calm. Wanda is high-energy, a social butterfly, and always on the go; she also loves to talk. These are all traits she inherited from our parents. In fact, all of my siblings are very social and embrace the diversity of life. We love all people.

Hearing the word "cancer" devastated Wanda. She felt better after the initial shock and knew I would be fine because of her experience with friends who are breast cancer survivors. Wanda was generally familiar with the treatment process. She understood that having breast cancer was not a death sentence and that aggressive treatment is critical to a successful outcome. Wanda said, "Your diagnosis wasn't only about you because your process involved all of the family." Within a matter of days after Claudette's phone calls, Wanda, Paula, and Fred had made plane reservations to be with me during my biopsy. What a blessing!

Once Wanda learned of my treatment plan, she said her role, apart from being my older sister, would be that of a strong support system. She started researching information on breast cancer so she could give me advice. Wanda, like Paula, would also send me beautiful prayers and inspirational verses to keep my spirits up. I especially thank her for the angel gift she sent me. It reminded me that she, Paula, Claudette, and Dale were my angels and would keep me in their constant prayers.

Wanda said my experience made her pay more attention to breast self-exams. Up until now, the only time she thought about breast exams was when she had her annual mammogram. After sharing with all my sisters that my tumor was estrogen-driven, Wanda and Claudette discontinued estrogen use. Paula continues to take estrogen pills, mainly to eliminate hot flashes. Paula is being closely monitored by her physician to ensure that she does not exceed the maximum length of recommended time.

Wanda called Dale to inform him that I had discovered a lump in my right breast. He lives in Topeka, Kansas, where we were all born and raised. Dale is a tall, handsome man with a warm demeanor. He is a people person, and everybody in Kansas seems to know him. Dale is a natural-born leader, not only in our family, but also in his long career in the Topeka educational system and within the Topeka community. While Dale is very social, he can also be shy. He is the kindest, most generous person I know. God so blessed me with Dale as my brother.

After talking to Wanda, Dale immediately wanted to know if he should come to Maryland along with my older twin sisters and brother-in-law for my biopsy surgery. Knowing his hectic schedule as the principal of our high school in Topeka and his other community commitments, I encouraged Dale not to come. I promised to update him and his wife, Anita, of my biopsy results. Strangely enough, I somehow knew that my lump was cancerous, but I didn't tell them.

Dale visited Claudette and me around the middle of November 2009, as I was finishing my last chemotherapy treatment. Dale's visit gave me such a wonderful uplift. I realized even more that spending time with family was strong medicine.

My diagnosis had a strong impact on Dale, primarily because all of us siblings had been fairly healthy with no major health concerns. Dale said, "I was saddened by the news of your diagnosis. I took the news hard about your surgeries and treatments you had to endure." Although he knew everything was in God's hands, he still hoped that I would be okay. While Dale is usually an optimistic person, he knew there was a possibility of things turning out otherwise. He and his wife Anita were very nervous about my situation. Dale was in constant prayer for his baby sister.

Initially, Dale was uncomfortable opening up about his fears and concerns during my process. He said, "I feel that sometimes, when one talks to people about their circumstances, it can be a reminder of things in one's own life that are difficult to deal with." Dale suffered a heart attack years ago, so it is understandable that he feels this way. Not knowing about all I was going through, Dale was reluctant to share his thoughts. He did not want to pile any more anxiety on my plate by talking about it. Dale is so thoughtful.

Dale was right; several times, I felt I could not possibly process anything more, especially when I was informed that my job was eliminated while I was on medical leave. Because my colleagues were deeply concerned about me, my phone rang constantly. They worried that the stress of battling breast cancer and losing my job would be overwhelming. I did my very best to reassure them that I would be all right.

It was at this point that I surrendered all my worries to God, and then I began to heal. I understood completely that it was God who designed my path in life and not me or anyone else. My complete acceptance of God allowed me to support and inspire coworkers whose jobs were also eliminated. It also empowered me to reach out to women who were experiencing a similar breast cancer journey. Wow, thank you, God. I listened.

My situation caused Dale to consider his own mortality as well as that of others close to him. He said to me, "Sis, until now, we have been blessed not to have had any real life-threatening emergencies among us. Here comes your situation that kind of reminds us of when dad had cancer, which led to his passing over. I think about my own mortality and the value of family and relationships." Dale and Anita were constantly checking on me and talking to my other siblings to find out how I was really getting along.

Anita, affectionately known as "Bunny," was caught off guard by my news. Anita is a wonderful sister-in-law whom we all love. She is kind, sensitive, and a good listener; she loves to take family photos and be my Lifetime Movie Network buddy.

A few weeks before Christmas, right after I finished my chemotherapy treatments, I remembered Anita sent me an angel ornament for our Christmas tree. The ornament featured my mother's picture where the angel's face would be. Another Christmas ornament presented a wedding picture of my parents. Anita doesn't know how deeply she touched my heart with these precious gifts which made me feel closer to my parents, who are resting in God's kingdom. I missed my parents, especially as I was battling this disease. My dad's strength and my mother's compassion are a strong part of who I am. God, I am ever so grateful for the blessing of my loving parents.

Anita said, "After the initial shock of hearing your diagnosis, it put everything in perspective. I realized that, due to advanced research, technology, and modern medicine, hope is much greater than in the past." Still, she and Dale were concerned about the procedures and side effects and uncertain about what more I'd have to endure. Once they'd heard from me and learned how well I seemed to be coping, they were more relaxed.

She would always say to me that it's okay to share your pain and that you don't have to be so strong all the time. There were certainly times when Byrd and I were not really clear on what was going on with me. As such, we decided not to share everything about my status until we knew exactly what was happening. I did not want our family to go through any more anxiety than necessary.

Anita is very supportive and a good listener. She hid her worry during my surgeries and treatments. She did not want to take the focus off of me by being upset and concerned. Once she realized that many more women today are surviving breast cancer, she gained a renewed sense of hope for my situation.

My health crisis made her realize she has to take the utmost care of her body and be more vigilant about seeing a doctor and following up when she suspects something is wrong. She also became aware of other people close to her who may experience health challenges. Anita said, "The best we can do when those challenges come is to be supportive and have a positive attitude." Anita is my favorite sister-in-law, not to mention my only sister-in-law !

My goddaughter, Orieyama, affectionately known as "Orie," is like a daughter to me. She is a wonderful young lady who was a strong part of my process. My family is proud that Orieyama accepted our love while growing up, and her mother did a great job raising her. Orieyama told me, "You had such an integral role during my childhood. Your family's influence impacts the way I view the world today."

"After finding out you were diagnosed with breast cancer I was shocked," she said. "I remember the day you discovered something abnormal and how you brought it up in conversation with me. When you described how you found the growth and how the surrounding area responded to the mass, I realized that this may be much more serious than we could ever expect. Your reaction was also one of anxiety, but you were positive throughout the entire process. I remember walking away from the conversation with the feeling that this was something more than we both wanted to admit. I knew from the research and being around people who have dealt with breast cancer that, if caught early in the process, the chances for survival were higher. I prayed that this would be the case and that, in the end, your life's path would become a living testimony to others. This made me feel a little more secure about the whole situation."

Orieyama was apprehensive to share things because she didn't want her thoughts to impact me. Her goal was to stay positive because the mind plays an important role in ensuring that we spring back from life's minor setbacks. She said, "Your positive attitude has amazed me so much over the years. Although positivity a characteristic I have always wanted, I haven't quite learned how to attain that goal yet.

"We have shared many talks over the years, and you have always told me that I remind you of an old soul in a little person's body. I had already experienced the loss of someone near and dear to me to cancer. After getting through that process, I thought I was free and clear, but not even a year later I found myself facing that 'C' word again with another person close to me. It was then that I realized that the wounds of the past had not yet healed. I try not to grow bitter with God, and I constantly seek answers for why this happened again. I was tired physically and mentally. My spirit was weak, and I thought that I had nothing left to give."

Orieyama and I worked for the same employer. Sometimes she would hear updates about my condition which I had not shared directly with her. I knew it was frustrating for her that people on my staff had information regarding my status before she did. Some people in my work unit just knew my schedule for doctor appointments and treatments.

At this point, Orieyama reminded herself that she was not a child anymore and could hold her own as an adult in our relationship. "I decided that I would be your sounding board, confidante, friend, or shoulder to cry on if you needed one," she said. "I knew that not every day would be good and that this would be more than a hill to climb. However, if I could be in your corner to help see you through, then I would. If I needed to be there in your moments of doubt and anguish, I would make a way."

Orieyama was my pillar of strength. She knew I was devastated when I told her about my lump. She became a solid rock for me when I didn't know if I was coming or going. Orieyama understood perfectly how much Byrd, Allan, and Warren meant to me and that the threat of the unknown was heartbreaking.

Orieyama told me, "Your situation impacted my life by allowing me to see God's power, strength, and love shine through the people who cared for you. I couldn't imagine life without you, and I wasn't willing to go down without fighting for you. Your experience allowed me to see that the journey with cancer doesn't always have to end in sadness. There is a reason you made it through. See, throughout the process, I prayed that you would be a living testament unto God and share your story with others who may be going through something similar. This experience has enhanced you, and you will never be the same. I thank you for sharing your walk with me."

This acknowledgement would not be complete without including Beverly Jo, who is my family's oldest and dearest friend. We grew up together in Topeka. Beverly Jo and I were born six months apart. As children, we were inseparable. When Beverly Jo relocated to California, we kept in touch. She is like a sister to my siblings and me. Her high energy, loving spirit, and generosity have always been appreciated.

When I asked Beverly Jo about her initial reaction to my diagnosis, She said, "I was devastated at first. I quickly felt comfort, though, because my mom had been a twenty-year breast cancer survivor, and I knew that you had a positive outlook." Beverly Jo said that in her heart, she knew I would survive. The most difficult part of my illness for Beverly Jo was that she could not be in Cheverly to comfort me during the treatments and my healing process.

She said, "I firmly believe that having a strong faith in God and knowing He will take care of you are key factors for healing completely." Beverly Jo prayed frequently and put my successful recovery in God's hands. She gave me much-needed support, as we talked regularly. I always felt her love. Beverly Jo was grateful that I shared my journey with her because it made her even more aware of how precious time is. She does not take anything in life for granted, and now she lives life to the fullest. Beverly Jo is my loving sister, and I will always cherish our love and friendship. I look forward to continuing on this wonderful journey together. I send much love to my sister in spirit.

Last but not least is our newly found cousin and neighbor, Ena Rochelle. Ena and her husband, Anthony, have three wonderful sons. Our backyards face each other, so we don't have far to go to see each other. Ena has always been a good friend, but I had a persistent hunch that she felt more like family. It wasn't until my husband Byrd and I went to Ena's mother's funeral that we found out Ena and Byrd are cousins. Wow! Talk about life's unexpected blessings. She loves the Lord and is very nurturing, kind, and fun; she also loves children. Our families are very close.

When I asked Ena for her initial reaction after learning of my diagnosis, she said, "Wow." She felt that God was preparing me to serve Him and that I was being transformed through my own strength.

"God, throughout Nia's journey, You left me in awe," she proclaimed. God blesses each of us with special gifts. He used Ena to minister to me before my breast cancer was even revealed. I believe God sent her to be one of my guardian angels. God tested Ena's strength after she lost her mother to cancer a year prior to my diagnosis. She did not know if she felt strong enough to be a part of my process. However, God gave her what she needed to be a constant for me, sharing her strength and acknowledgement of God's word. She said that I encouraged her to be open with her emotions after she witnessed me persevere through my battle with cancer. Ena took what she learned from her mother's experience with cancer and applied it to me. She understands that life is precious and she wants to create positive experiences for those she cares about. Ena believed that my positivity and strong desire to learn more about God's word would be the beginning of my spiritual breakthrough.

My situation impacted Ena's own life. She said, "I look at you as a big sister, a mentor, and I want to be like you. The strength you demonstrated was very inspiring. I now embrace both the positive and challenging experiences in life and see these as opportunities to learn and grow as a better mom, wife, and friend. Blessings do come unexpectedly. You trust God that this is His path for you and that all things work together for the good."

Friends:

Beverly is the most wonderful person whom I have ever known in my life. She is the godmother to our sons. We met through our husbands, Byrd and Tony, who first met at a music concert many years ago. Beverly had two daughters, Kali and Kim. Her oldest daughter, Kim, passed away in January 2009 from kidney disease.

Kim was my inspiration because of her strength, determination, and zest for life. She said to me before she passed away, "Nia, you will be just fine because you are so strong and positive." Kim truly inspired me as I watched her desire and struggle to live. She truly gave me hope and encouragement. I believe that Kim's personality was like that of her father, who passed away before her. Kali, the youngest daughter, possesses a lot of her mother's qualities. Kali, too, is a champion for all the support and love she provided her sister and mother; they appreciated Kali's strength, more than she knows, during that difficult time.

While I missed Beverly's presence during my treatment, I understood completely. Still, Beverly frequently called to check on me. She was deeply concerned about both Kim and me. I admire Beverly for being a strong warrior for so many people in her life. She buried her husband, her mother, and her daughter, and yet she continued to embrace life to the fullest. She is an amazing woman—a true friend and hero. I know God has blessed our friendship forever.

Beverly said, "When I learned of your diagnosis with breast cancer, I was stunned and wondered how this could have happened to her good friend. I cried all that day." Because of her daughter's terminal illness, it was an emotional time for her. Once she cried and got over the sadness, Beverly knew that my losing the battle to cancer was not an option. A devoutly spiritual Buddhist, Beverly chanted daily that I would go right through this obstacle and that it would somehow be a tremendous benefit for me.

Beverly said my situation made her realize how precious life is. We have to experience joy at every moment and not get hung up on the small stuff. She added, "When born, we're going to die. But in between that time, we have to experience joy, have fun, and never ever give up on our dreams. That is one thing I say about Nia. She inspires me to dream big because it doesn't matter what happens; she will never give up on her dreams."

I learned from the best. Beverly has never viewed life as a problem, only an opportunity to grow. Her positive nature, fun-loving spirit and nurturing ways have always added value to my life. I will always cherish our lifelong friendship.

Lord, have mercy! Marilyn is a fireball—full of good, positive energy. In the midst of any storm, Marilyn may be making jewelry, cooking, writing a church article, or planning a trip. Sometimes she does them all at the same time. She is the ultimate multitasker.

God placed Marilyn in my life at the right time to help me understand what I would experience throughout my breast cancer journey. It was very comforting to be embraced by a friend who had a similar breast cancer experience. Marilyn reassured me and gave me hope, even though I knew she did not share certain experiences to spare me additional anxiety. Her experience as a breast cancer patient was different from mine because very few people knew of her journey. Marilyn said, "I did not share my journey seventeen years ago, but it was good to see you go through yours very openly. I have learned a lot through your process and can see the value of being open to help someone else along the way. Every journey is different and unique. But the good news is every breast cancer survivor has at least one thing in common: victory."

Marilyn recalled telling her daughter, Leah, of her anger at the doctor's uncertainty regarding my diagnoses. "It's frightening for a patient dealing with such a critical disease to learn that the disease is far more advanced than initially suspected. You don't know what's going on inside you. You rely upon your doctor to give you an accurate diagnosis. I can only imagine what Nia was going through after the doctors told her about the advanced stage."

Marilyn said, "I watched you get weak and tired, and ultimately lose your hair, I wondered what you were thinking about. You handled it a lot better than most people. The fact that you made us all laugh during this difficult time was great. However, we knew that you were in pain. You laughed about hair loss, bleeding gums, itchy skin, burning stomach, burned skin, and purchasing a wig. Sometimes you were laughing and carrying on so much, we forgot you were battling cancer. You found humor in every situation you encountered, including the car accident in the grocery store parking lot."

Truthfully humor was a must for getting through this process. Otherwise, this whole scenario would have been much different. Laughter is and always will be my healing medicine.

Carolyn has been a dear friend of mine for thirty years. She is a beautiful, positive, caring person who is loyal to and supportive of her family and friends. She retired from her career a year before I was diagnosed; she was devoted and committed to me during and after my journey.

Carolyn has been a tremendous blessing in my life. She was very afraid when Wanda shared my breast cancer diagnosis. She had never known anyone personally who had breast cancer, so it was difficult for her to hear about the treatments and see me at my worst. She tried her best to stay strong for me.

Carolyn was inspired by my positive attitude and my will to never give up. She said, "Your illness taught me that life can throw you some unexpected situations of which only God knows the outcome. In moving forward, I will embrace all that life sends me, good or otherwise."

My dear friend and co-worker, Pam, asked me if she could be a part of my treatment process. Pam is a beautiful young woman. A mother of two daughters, she is married, fun-loving, and direct yet sensitive. She and I had been co-workers for nearly ten years by that time.

Like others, Pam was very surprised to hear about my diagnosis. The sheer emotional weight of my diagnosis reminded her that she, too, was carrying a huge emotional load. She associated cancer with death. Pam later said, "Boy, was I wrong about you. You're back and better than ever! And while there were times I wanted to share my concerns, I felt that you had so much to deal with—regarding your own fears, family, and work—that I had to be strong for you. I was no stranger to dealing with a loved one battling cancer, having lost my mother. I just wanted us to continue having fun, and I wanted to be a sounding board for you as you continued to understand your illness.

"During our time together, I did not want to take things so seriously, but I also did not want to make light of the situation either. I wanted to accompany you to your treatments because I wanted that time with you and couldn't think of a better way to show my support. I knew you had lots of family and friends cooking and caring for you at home, so I knew you were okay in that way. I wanted us to have *sistah-girl* bonding time, like we had when we traveled for our company."

Pam and I made an awesome team because we took our work seriously and enjoyed it at the same time. Yes, Pam and I were truly blessed to have that kind of special relationship.

My situation had a profound impact on Pam's life as well. She told me, "You are the bravest person I know. The way you faced this challenge head-on and didn't allow yourself to collapse under the sheer weight of it all is a testament to your strength. You have shown me that not everything in life is easy, but how you deal with it builds character. I love, love, love you so much for that. You are an amazing woman.

You opened yourself and your family to me. My mother lost her battle to lung cancer at the tender age of forty-six, and my oldest sister died in a fatal car accident at the age of thirty-six. Those two major losses left me with a fear of taking risks in life, kept me from asserting myself and from loving others, and even made me keep people at a distance to avoid total devastation should something happen. You taught me that it's okay to love again, to be a free spirit, and to take risks. You have filled the void left by the loss of my mother in so many ways. I look to you for the love and encouragement that I missed so dearly by not having my mom and my sister around. I have learned to cherish every moment with my kids and to live bravely."

My spiritual healing was bolstered by the positive outlooks of those around me. Terri, my spiritual friend, accompanied me to a session. Our time together was very special because it gave me the opportunity to join in fellowship with Terri.

Quite frankly, I looked forward to the chemotherapy treatment sessions because they offered the only time that I could eat without incident. Normally, my stomach would not tolerate most of the foods I enjoyed. Immediately after the chemotherapy sessions, my appetite was up and I was able to eat practically anything. And I did. My friends and I would use this opportunity to continue bonding, visit different restaurants, and enjoy wonderful meals.

Prilla, a friend who was with me throughout my entire process, was also born and raised in Topeka. But I didn't get to know her until I moved to Washington. We have been friends ever since. Prilla is like a surrogate big sister to me. She has a daughter named Nicole, and I am Nicole's surrogate aunt. I love them dearly. When the three of us get together, we laugh the night away. We cook, dance, fix each other's hair, and just have a lot of fun. I can always count on my girls!

Prilla's initial reaction to my diagnosis was fear and then lots of questions. She said, "I was afraid that I might lose a friend whom I was not ready to be without." She asked, "How could this happen to such an active, vibrant person, who seemed to have the best of life awaiting her? I feared the outcome. I've known others who've succumbed to the disease shortly after the diagnosis. I did not want that to happen to Claudean. There seemed to be so many things I wanted to talk to her about; she couldn't leave without these talks taking place. I wanted to give her encouragement and learn from the strength she displayed. My only worry was that she was taking on too much and not taking time for herself. On many occasions, I mentioned that she needed to allow time for rest. Clearly, she did not listen."

Prilla was correct; I didn't listen. While there were moments I had no choice, I couldn't seem to rest during my wellness process. In the past, I only required about five to six hours of sleep to function and feel good. I never was a person to sleep a lot or take naps. Even though the illness should have prompted me to rest more, the pain did not always allow me to do so. My personality is such that positive energy becomes my medicine, and being around so many wonderful people seemed to energize me.

Prilla told me that, whatever she may face in life, she hopes to have the same strength and courage that I had to get through it. She hopes to slow down, concentrate on herself, and make her health the number one priority. Prilla is a loving, sensitive, and caring friend. I have thoroughly enjoyed our conversations filled with laughter, which often leave us both crying uncontrollably. I can talk to her about anything and everything. I am so blessed to have her in my life. Prilla was 100 percent there for me during my difficult time, and I hope I will be able to serve her as dutifully as she did me.

My dear friend Louise was available on several occasions, not only to accompany me to a chemotherapy session but also to come with me to other doctor appointments. Louise and I are very good friends; we were brought together by our sons about twelve years ago. Louise's family is an extension of my family. We vacation together, share holiday dinners, and enjoy each other's company. My youngest son, Allan, and Louise and Mike's son, Bryant, are like brothers. Allan also inherited a surrogate sister, Sabrina, the daughter of Louise and Mike.

Louise was scared, sad, and worried upon learning of my breast cancer diagnosis. Louise knew she would be able to cope with my illness and treatments because she felt my faith and strength would sustain me. She was encouraged by my faith and hope, and she was heartened by the group of friends that embraced me with so much love. Louise was completely available to support me throughout my journey. My journey taught her to be faithful and to prioritize taking care of herself.

I asked Monica about her initial reaction after I shared my diagnosis with her (at work, mind you). The news was shocking, and she felt fearful that our budding relationship might be affected. She said she prayed that God wouldn't take me away. Most people who receive a diagnosis of breast cancer are caught off-guard, and the shock can lead to depression. She was impressed by my handling of the diagnosis. "Your positive attitude reinforced to me that everything was going to be okay, and that this was another obstacle that you would have to overcome in life," she said.

Monica has had surgery nine times due to an abnormality of her kidneys. She indicated that, as she was going through that process, her husband, Lake, was very supportive, which kept her spirits up. Likewise, Monica wanted to be a support system for me. "I felt your pain and knew that you would need all the support you could get. Some who experience breast cancer do not survive because they give up too early, fearing the fight to get rid of the disease."

When I asked Monica how my situation impacted her life, she told me, "My mother-in-law passed away shortly before I met you. She was very much a mother figure for me. She had a kind spirit and always looked at life in the most positive way. After she died, I felt like a lost puppy. I truly believe God puts people in our lives for a reason, and you were put in my life to give me the positive reinforcement that I needed. There have been many times when I wanted to think negatively about various situations, but in our many conversations, you have brought that positive spirit back to me. I have learned that I need to put more faith in God and trust that He will take care of my family.

"Your illness has taught me to keep my head up because life is short, and we must enjoy it while we are on this earth. Like you mentioned to me before, 'There's no need to get down about it; you just get through it and keep on movin'!' Thank you for being such a wonderful inspiration in my life." Monica was an unexpected surprise in my life as well. She and her family are truly wonderful people. I will always cherish our relationship, with or without hair.

Bernetta is a single mother. Her quiet, sensitive nature makes her stronger than she really knows. She was always available to run errands for me, accompany me to a chemotherapy session or an appointment, or just keep me company. Brandon, her son, visited me often, even without his mom; he was such a great little helper.

Bernetta was saddened to hear of my diagnosis. She wanted to help out wherever I had a need. She tried her best to maintain hope and a positive outlook while I was going through my treatments. Through my experience, she realized how short life is and that you don't know how many twists and turns it's going to take.

Cynthia and I have known each other for more than twenty years and have always been spiritual buddies. For several years now, Cynthia and I, along with several other wonderful women, have fellowshipped together at Zion Church and participated in a small group outside church services. Cynthia was most proud of the way God used me over the past four or five years since we started attending small group. She and her husband are next-door neighbors and very close friends. Both Cynthia and her husband, Oliver, were surprised and caught off guard upon hearing that I was diagnosed with breast cancer. Cynthia did not know what to say or how to react when I shared this with her because she and Oliver had just received word that a friend of theirs had died from breast cancer that day. I now understand why Cynthia's reaction to my diagnosis with breast cancer was so indifferent. She seemed so preoccupied and really didn't say much at all.

Oliver was concerned because of the high incidence of cancer on our street. As of this writing, three people on our block have died of cancer and another three were diagnosed with the disease—one with prostate cancer, one with brain cancer, and me with breast cancer. Life is awesome and yet unpredictable. You never know what God has in store or when change will occur in our lives.

Cynthia shared with me that she felt very confident in my relationship with God and knew He was going to use me in a manner to serve people. She said, "There were times I was worried about the outcome of your illness. However, watching you go through your wellness process was a great lesson for me."

My situation made Cynthia more aware of cancer itself and how the disease affects people. Also, she became more aware of her own medical challenges and realized that no day is promised to anyone. For Oliver, my illness reminded him of how fragile life is. I send them lots of love and thank them for being there for my family and me.

My friend Anita and I both have a twin, so we share this uncommon experience. I met Anita through her husband, David, who is my brother's best friend. I have known Anita for more than thirty years. We have laughed and shopped together, and we have motivated and encouraged each other throughout our friendship. One of our proudest moments was earning our bachelor's degrees after raising our children. Each year, we set goals and share them with each other. We have always shared our dreams and held each other accountable for achieving them.

When I shared my diagnosis with Anita, she said a prayer refusing to claim the disease. Because of my positive energy, Anita believed the outcome would be successful. She felt that God would not take me away. Anita is familiar with the breast cancer process because her mother battled the disease. Unfortunately, she succumbed to breast cancer. One difference, Anita believed, is that I maintained a positive outlook throughout the entire process. Until the day she passed away, Anita's mom remained bitter about the disease and the toll it took on her and her family. My optimism gave Anita hope that my outcome would be different.

Anita knows the importance of having a strong belief in God and understanding that, with faith, all things are possible. Anita believed I would heal and fully recover because of my strength and faith in God. She knew her friend would be all right. I love Anita, and she has always been like a sister to me as we have both raised our families and continued to develop ourselves. I look forward to many more adventures together.

Pat is a wonderful girlfriend, partner in crime, and next-door neighbor. We are always there for each other. Pat reminded me that we have known each other since 1992 when, she says, I warmly welcomed her with open arms into the Cheverly neighborhood. It would be unfair to mention Pat without mention of her husband, Larry. They both have been wonderful neighbors and were very supportive friends during that time.

While I was going through the chemotherapy treatments, they made sure I had everything I needed to be comfortable at home. It seemed that every time I ran out of Tums to settle my stomach indigestion, Pat was calling me to say, "Open the door; Larry is bringing you some more Tums." They also maintained a constant flow of flavored popsicles for my sore throat, as well as broth, juices, and many other food items. Pat and Larry never missed a beat. I thank them both for being so sensitive to my needs.

Pat told me of her devastation upon learning of my breast cancer diagnosis. "I was crestfallen," she said. "After I hung up the telephone, I just sat there quietly for about an hour, pondering and praying and hoping for a good outcome. I was really stunned at the news but amazed at how you came to find the lump in your breast. I believe it was God that led you, in the middle of the night, to examine yourself and make that discovery. That was a blessing. Still, it was very disturbing news, and it did throw me for a loop."

Pat added, "Although the treatment process was grueling, it wasn't difficult hearing about the surgeries, treatments, and healing. In times like these, support is critical, and my only concern was that I was not more available to you. During this time, it wasn't about me. It was about you and the extent to which I could be there emotionally and physically to help you with whatever you needed. I got over my own worries; I wasn't the one going through the experience."

I asked Pat how my illness and wellness journey impacted her life. "Well, first, it was inspirational to see how you went through the process," she said. "And you had such an extensive network of wonderfully supportive family and friends. Seeing everyone come through for you was so amazing. The one thing that I reflected on periodically was that I was still a cigarette smoker, and I have known that I obviously needed to stop way before you took ill. Your illness did drive that point home for me.

"I was most impressed with the graceful manner in which you went through your process, as difficult as it was. I was also grateful that you allowed those of us who care about you to participate and be of some assistance to you. Whether a person who is ill believes it or not, by allowing others to be involved in the care giving, he or she can help others understand and learn to cope with the illness."

Pat is absolutely right. I believe the opportunity to learn sometimes happens unexpectedly. These opportunities bring people together and deepen our faith in God. Friends don't get any better than Pat and Larry. I send much love to them both for being such good folks.

Monee was shocked after finding out I was diagnosed with breast cancer. She didn't have a lot of experience dealing with an illness such as mine. "I had a great-grandmother and a stepmother-in-law who were sick, and I think what was surprising to me was how well you handled the process," Monee shared. She found my process difficult, not because of me, but because it reminded her of some past experiences with her stepmother-in-law and her great-grandmother. Although she may have felt compassion, she did not have the opportunity to show much of it when they were ill; so my illness and wellness journey offered an opportunity for her to really grow and be as supportive as she could. As we know, God works in many wonderful ways.

Like we had always done, Monee felt that we could talk about anything and everything, and communicating during this time was no different for her. She shared that my illness and healing cautioned her to be more attentive toward cancer patients and their needs and emotions. Also, she recognized that my illness made me realize the importance of faith in God. "Even though you were going through it, so many people that I spoke with and talked to could see how you rose above the circumstances and trusted God. Your growth in faith was evident for all to witness," she said.

My path to God certainly changed when I met Monee and became a part of Transition, her small life group through the church. Timing is everything. I know that my situation was simply God's way of preparing me for the next chapter in my life.

I realized that my path was His, and that He was ready for me to get back on His course for my life. I send much love to my friend, Monee.

Barbara, whom I affectionately call "BK," gave me a special, precious gift during my illness and wellness. Her baby boy, Zarin, lifted me up every time she brought him over to my house. I looked forward to seeing Zarin and holding him in my arms. The love of her sweet baby was great therapy while going through this difficult time.

Barbara said, "You are so wise, and you have a warm and inviting personality and a fabulous smile (especially when you laugh). You can be witty in an off-the-cuff kind of way; you have a tremendous sense of humor, and you are amazingly supportive of people's journeys toward success and personal fulfillment. Claudean, you are just an amazing woman and a gift to so many people." Through describing me, Barbara was describing herself also.

Barbara dreaded having to revisit her thoughts during the time of my diagnosis. With all the information available, she was well aware that, when detected early, the survival rate for breast cancer patients is high. But my tumor was already in an advanced stage. She was nervous and fearful and cautiously optimistic. But because I was being strong and focused on the upcoming aggressive treatment, she felt there was no time for sadness.

Overall, Barbara was rather relaxed during my treatment process. She had a general concern, but my attitude kept her at ease. Barbara said, "I knew there would be challenges, but I believed Claudean had excellent care, and I just felt at peace that her journey would be a successful one." My journey taught Barbara to be in tune with her own body's signals and vigilant about her health when it came to working with health care professionals.

In addition to positive relationships, spiritual healing was a powerful therapy throughout my journey. Spiritual healing restored my faith, gave me hope for a positive future, and connected me to friends and family. So you see, this book could not have been written without a tribute to the love and support of my family and friends.

After my treatment process, I learned that everyone supporting me needed to heal from this devastating situation or from a different circumstance that they experienced while supporting me.

My family and friends kept me anchored and feeling safe and secure. I never felt alone because I was so richly cared for during this vulnerable time, and that helped me to embrace my journey. Family and friends encouraged me never to give up. They were the healing medicine that contributed to my successful recovery.